NEWBURGH
Portrait of a City

Dmitri Kasterine

NEWBURGH

Portrait of a City

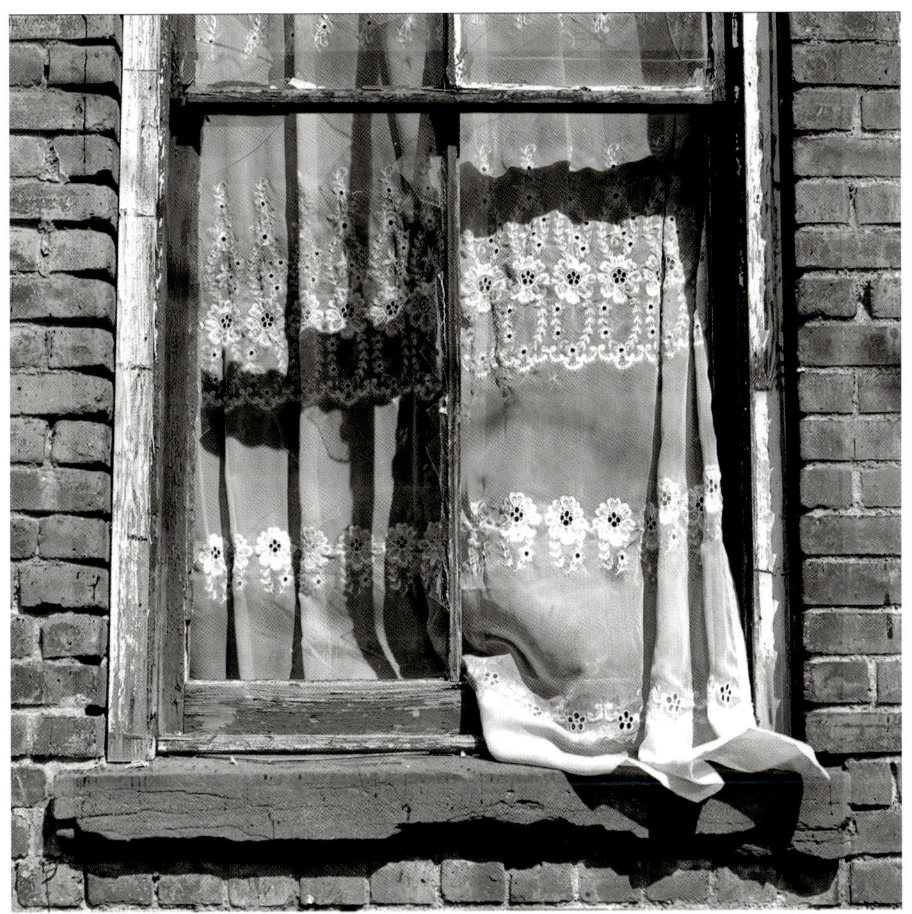

PREFACE BY DAVID DASCH

The Quantuck Lane Press
New York

For Caroline

Design by Laura Lindgren
Manufacturing by Mondadori Printing, Verona

Printed in Italy
First Edition

Library of Congress Cataloging-in-Publication Data
Kasterine, Dmitri.
Newburgh : portrait of a city / Dmitri Kasterine ; preface by David Dasch. — 1st ed.
p. cm.
1. Newburgh (N.Y.)—Pictorial works. I. Title.
F129.N7K37 2012
974.7'31—dc23 2012005099

The Quantuck Lane Press, New York
www.quantucklanepress.com

Distributed by
W. W. Norton & Company
500 Fifth Avenue
New York, NY 10110
www.wwnorton.com

W. W. Norton & Company Ltd.
Castle House
75/76 Wells Street
London, WIT 3QT

1 2 3 4 5 6 7 8 9

PREFACE

From our throne of hindsight the decline looks inexorable, a systemic whittling away of commerce and connection. As was the case in cities across America, and particularly in many cities in the Hudson Valley in the 1950s and increasingly so in the 1960s, Newburgh was trapped in something like a cruel game of musical chairs, played out in societal breadth, with one opportunity after another taken away from those determined to play on.

The story has a numbing familiarity of a clock. Industry unraveled, the infrastructure of factories came undone, with resulting radial decay of small business. Malls proliferated along lengthening automotive corridors, further wrenching vitality from the inner city. Increasingly constricted, the sub-normalized middle class saw no chance but to go, leaving behind those with virtually no choice but to stay, as more of the impoverished were drawn into the breach from elsewhere.

Much of the city's nineteenth century architectural heritage perished; renewal projects foundered. Vagrancy, anger, and crime corroded neighborhoods recut by gang geography. To this day, federal authorities slice through these neighborhoods on crime raids. However, at the turn of this century, as other diminished cities were giving evidence of a renewal paradigm at work, so Newburgh seemed to be clawing its way to rebuilding and restoration. As raw, reduced and vast as this city is, the turning has been halting and lured to false starts, yet there is an abiding hope that this will be a true turning nonetheless.

It was a tip from an acquaintance that led Dmitri Kasterine to venture into Newburgh. What he encountered there tugged at him again and again, though inexplicably at first. Yet that connection between photographer and photograph is often inexplicable, and indeed it should be so. In his 1981 collection *England and the English* Kasterine wrote of that moment when a charged sensibility flares upon encountering the subject discovered:

> A picture can appear almost anywhere, so not too much planning. Just going along, awake, seeing… Nothing stands out so far, nothing I haven't

seen before, nothing that sends a cold shiver down my back. Then I see it! There it is… Yes. The feeling. Without it, nothing, just a record. There, done it… Yes. Terrific! Got it. The tension subsides.

Dynamic with decline and assertion, Newburgh proved to be generous with such moments.

Born in England in 1932, Kasterine at age eleven was photographing birds at his mother's feeder. Now his career encompasses nearly five decades of work for magazines, advertising agencies, corporations and the film industry. Especially in his portraiture and his landscapes there accrues that sublime abeyance of great photographs, by which his subjects, for being captured by his eye, are granted the freedom to display and even celebrate their uniqueness. His pictures have a stillness about them and a breath within them. We see this whether we're looking at his Queen of England or his Newburgh bar owner (page 43), his 1965 Beckett or his 1997 man with a scar on his shoulder (58) and his 1999 girl with scars on her stomach (87), his Stonehenge at twilight or his house on Lander Street with a hole in its roof (92).

So keenly unobtrusive is Kasterine's sensibility that even the severing edifices of Newburgh seem to be posing for him, at peace in camera time: the disused garage (102) and the parking lot turned vacant lot (12), the cars long ago driven away; the grande old dame house invaded by ailanthus trees (101), others suffocated by ivy (8, 52); doors tagged by numbers of mocking vestigial significance (52); and the once pulsing now a jumble of shapes Newburgh Paper Company factory, hung with awnings like shrouds (64).

Thoreau wrote that the mass of men lead lives of quiet desperation but the people of this battered cityscape afford the camera a great deal more. Is that the grain of desperation in the face of the woman holding the baby (68)? Perhaps it's there but so is love and resolve. If quiet desperation is in the eyes of the man from Jamaica (95), it is alloyed with a survivor's prudence. As the photographer focuses his camera, so does the subject his identity. Some treat the camera as a spotlight, and project a self-idealization with boundless conviction: those in their street livery who are claiming turf authority (17, 29, 31, 71, 74), the women who know the camera longs to look at them (16, 41). Others project self-possession from within a perimeter of faith and some guilelessly express an irrepressible grace through tenderness (45, 75, 91, 98). A woman sits on a couch in a welfare hotel (15). She is dominated by a mural, a tapestry of an old dream of a thriving 1950s Newburgh. A beautiful little girl twines her arm around a beautiful little boy's (69), their eyes free of the past. Dmitri Kasterine's portrait of Newburgh bares a city in anxious balance, and he so powerfully retrieves all these people for us that we can't do otherwise than hope the balance tips in their favor.

David Dasch

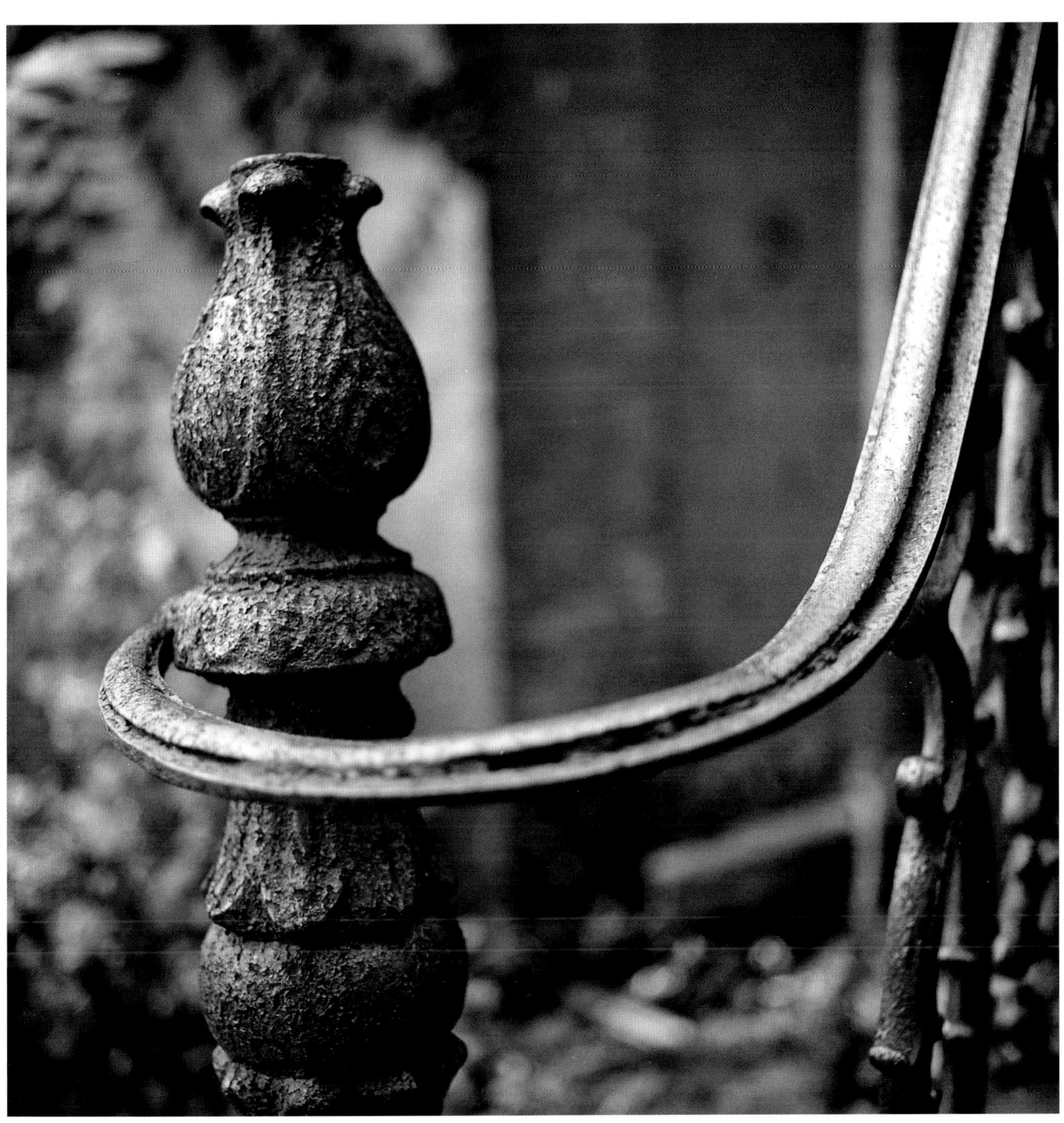

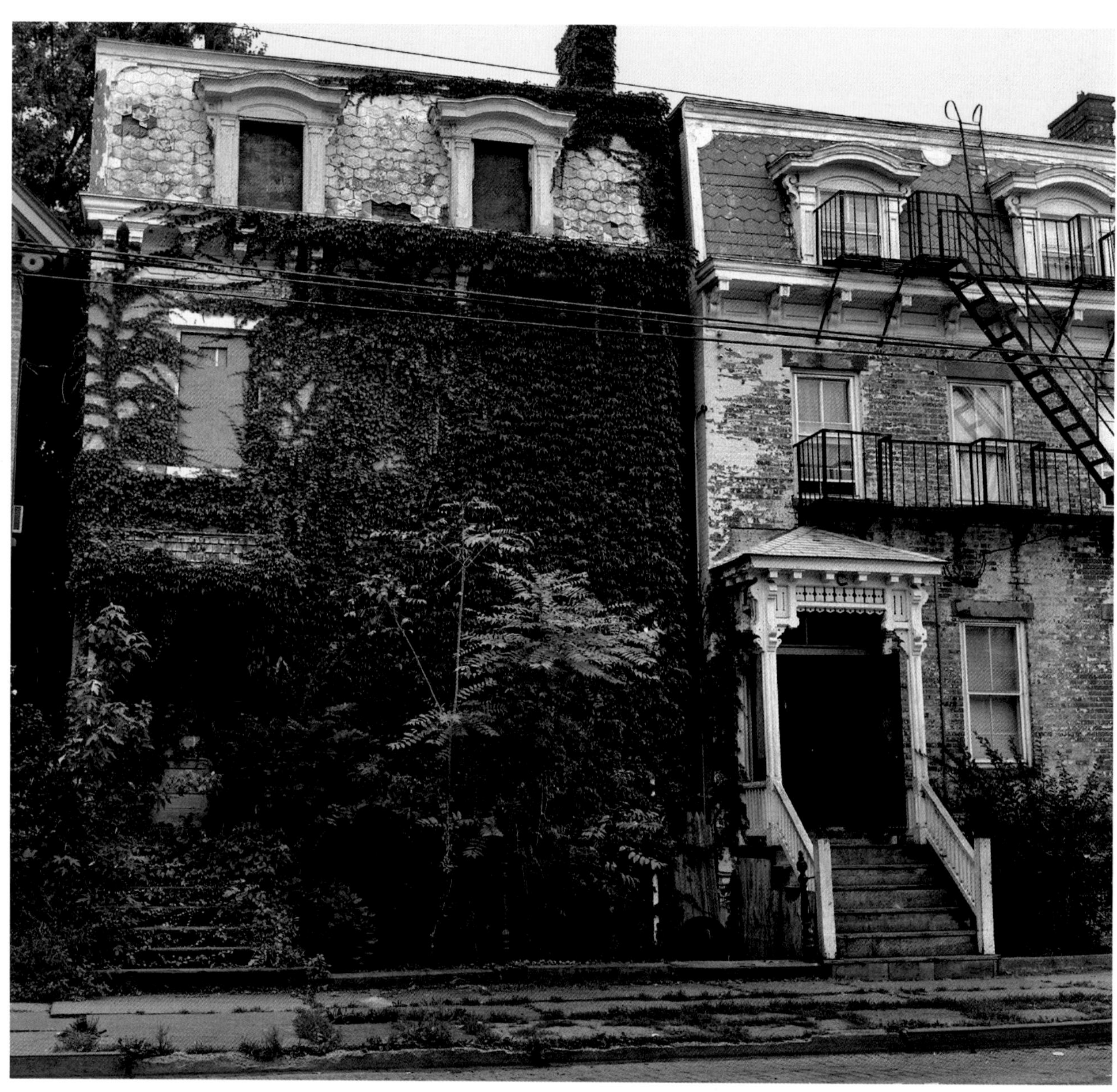

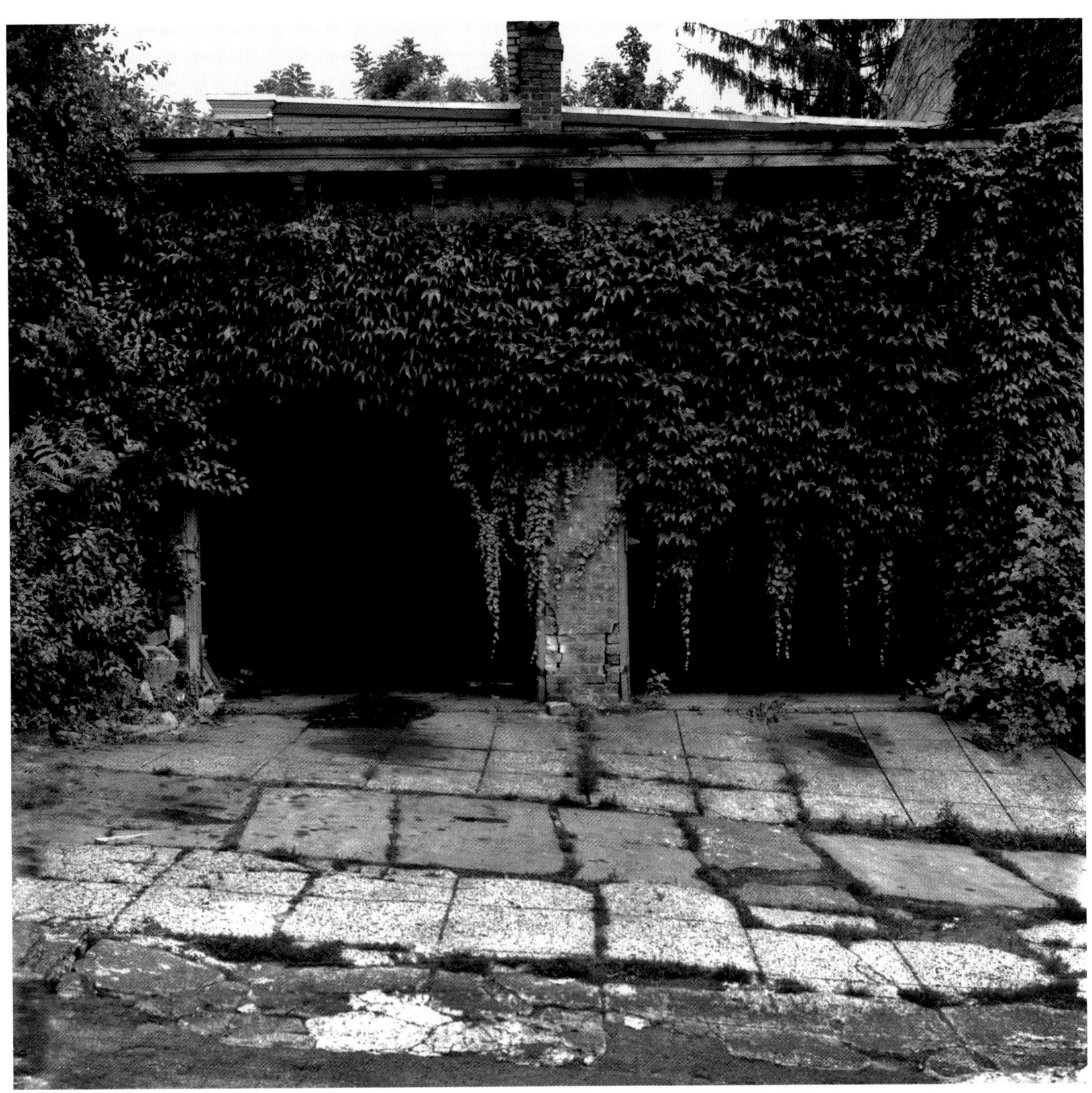

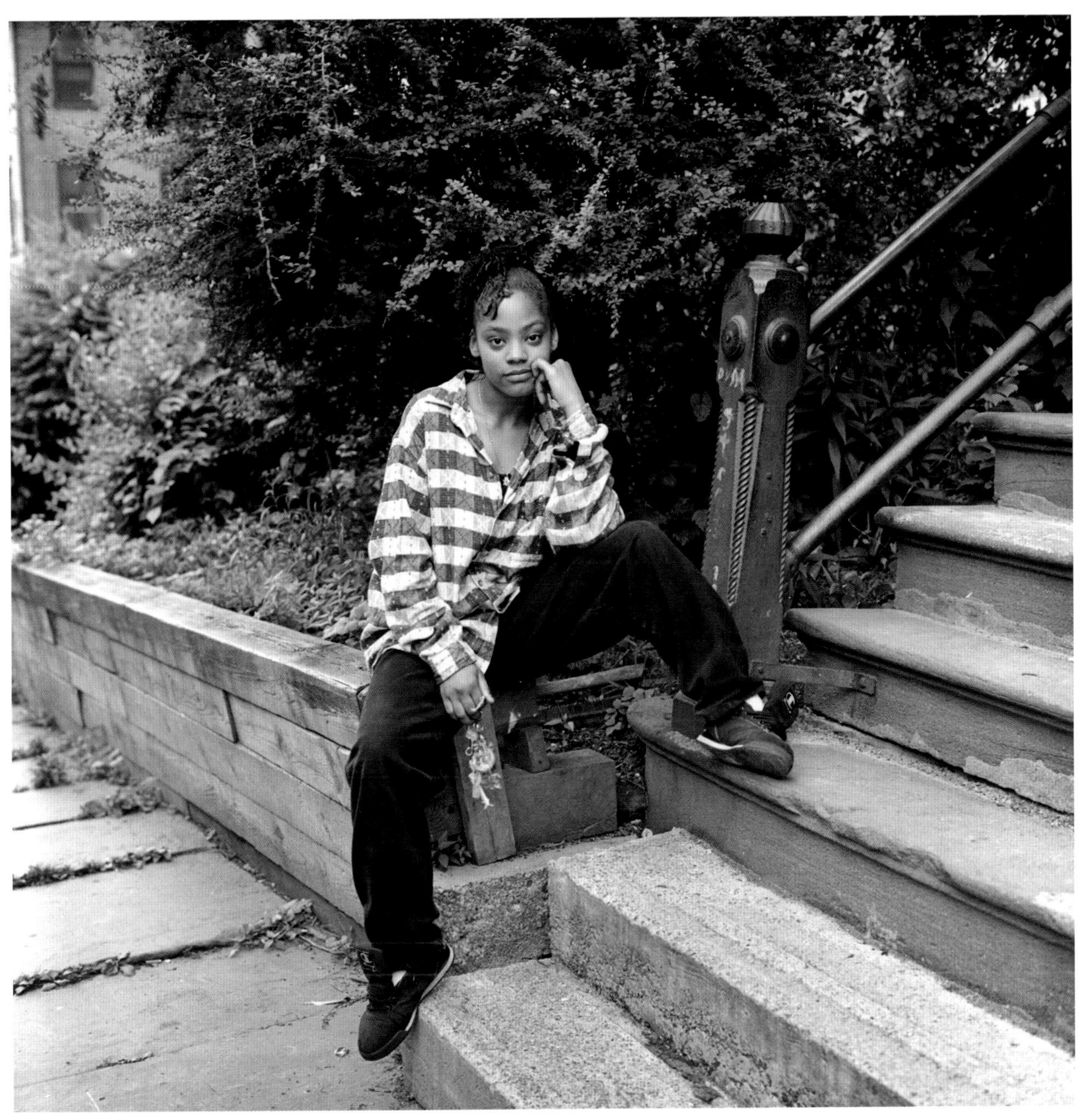

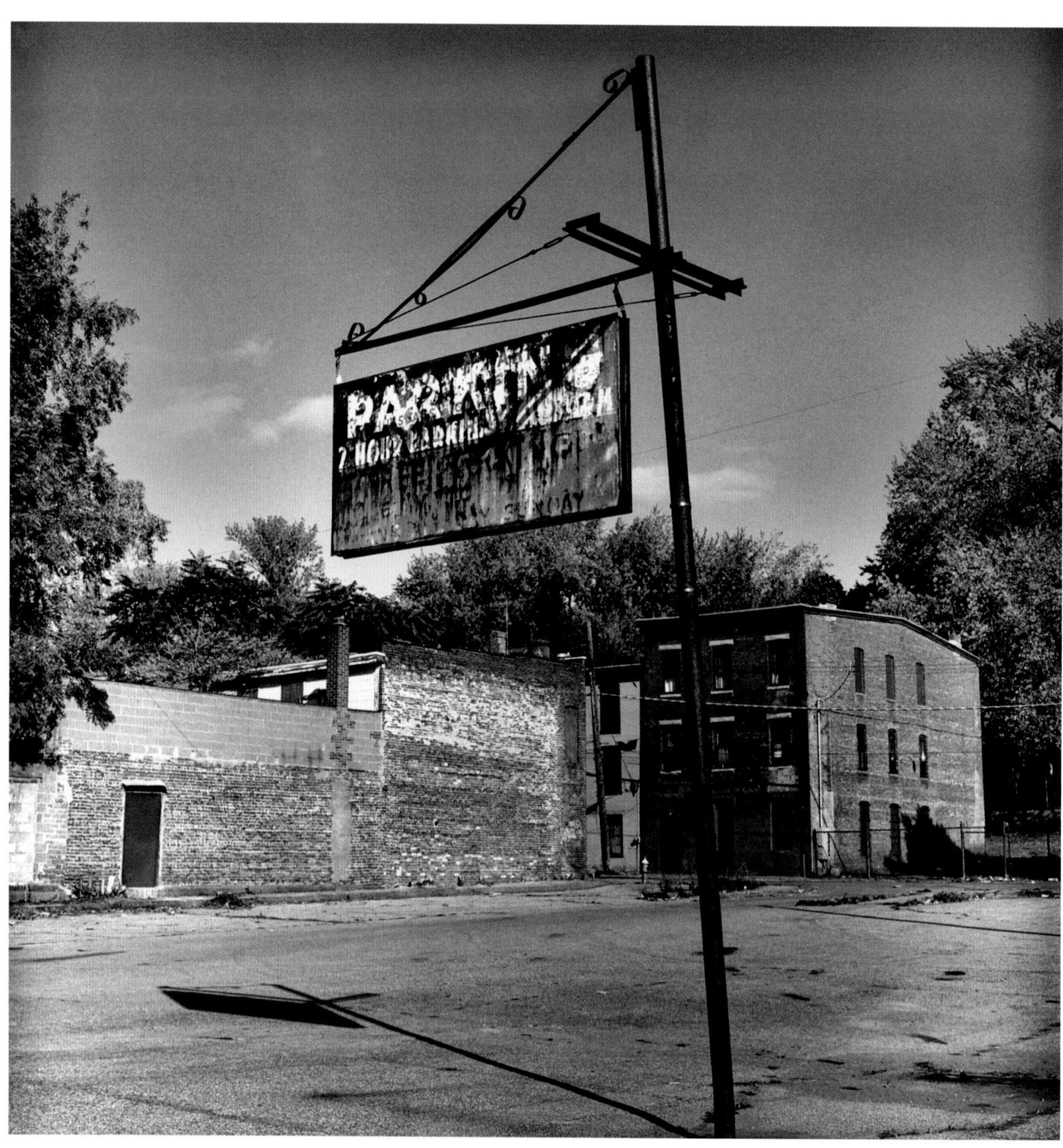
PARKING
2 HOUR

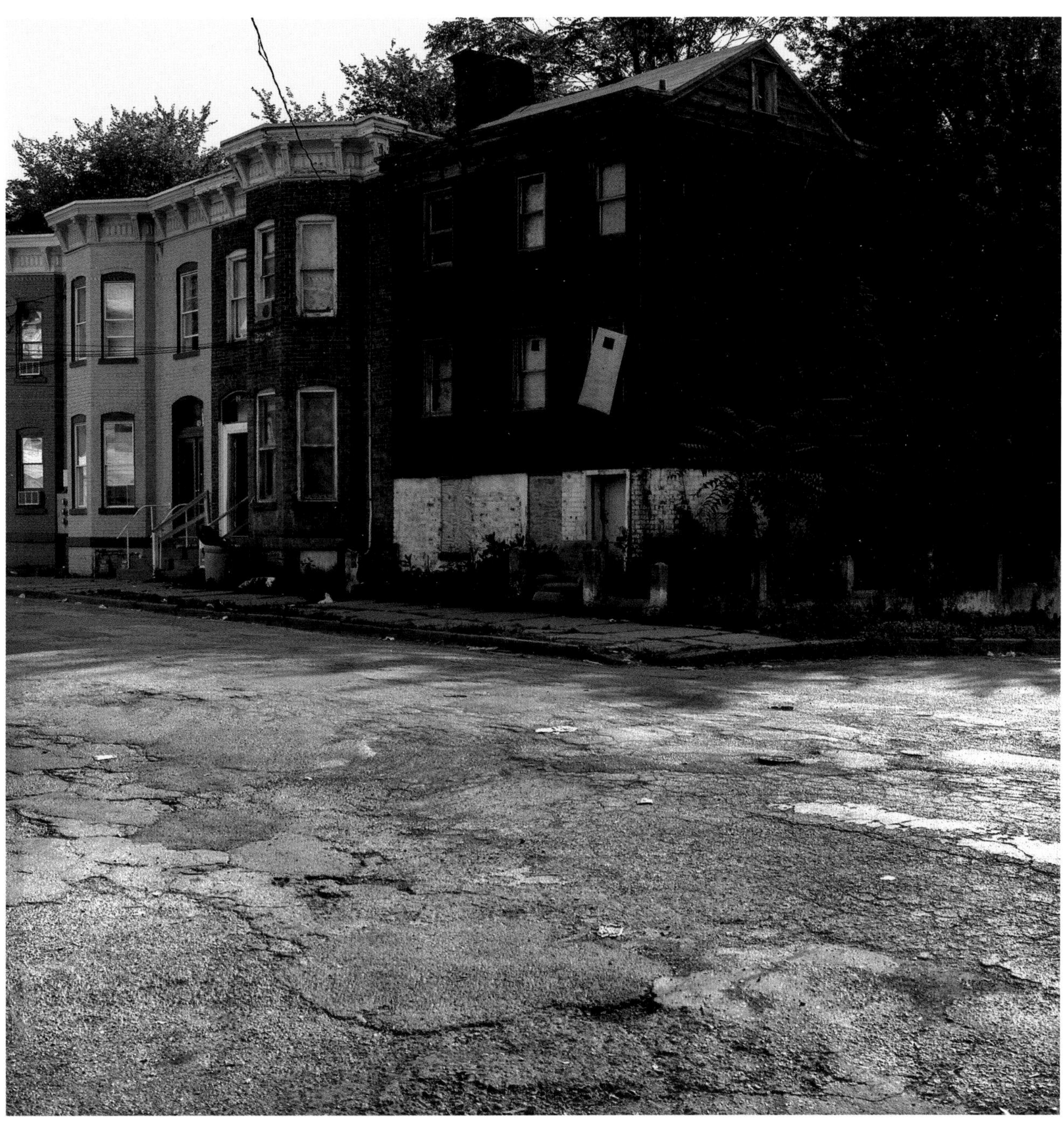

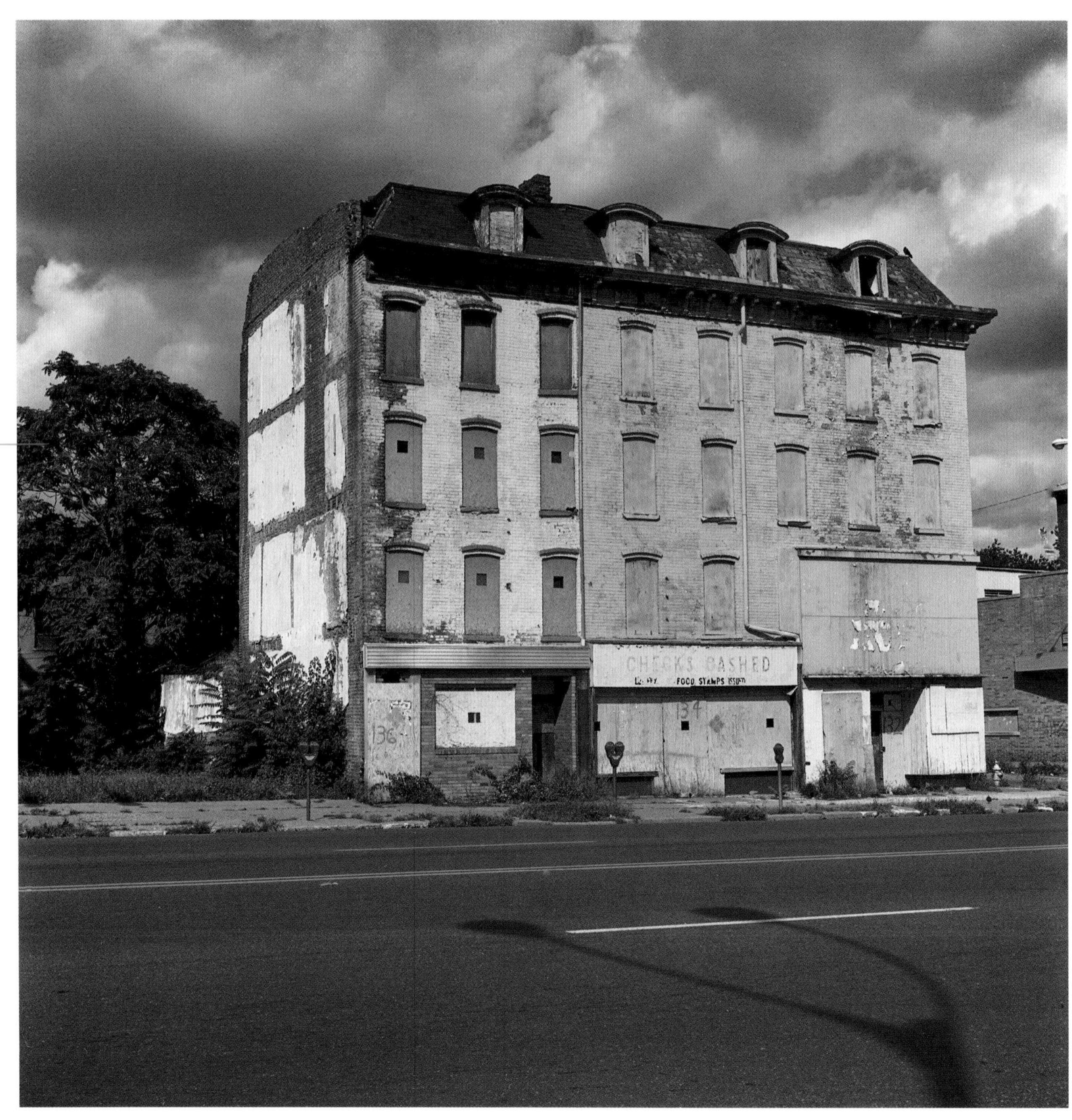
CHECKS CASHED
FOOD STAMPS ISSUED
136
134

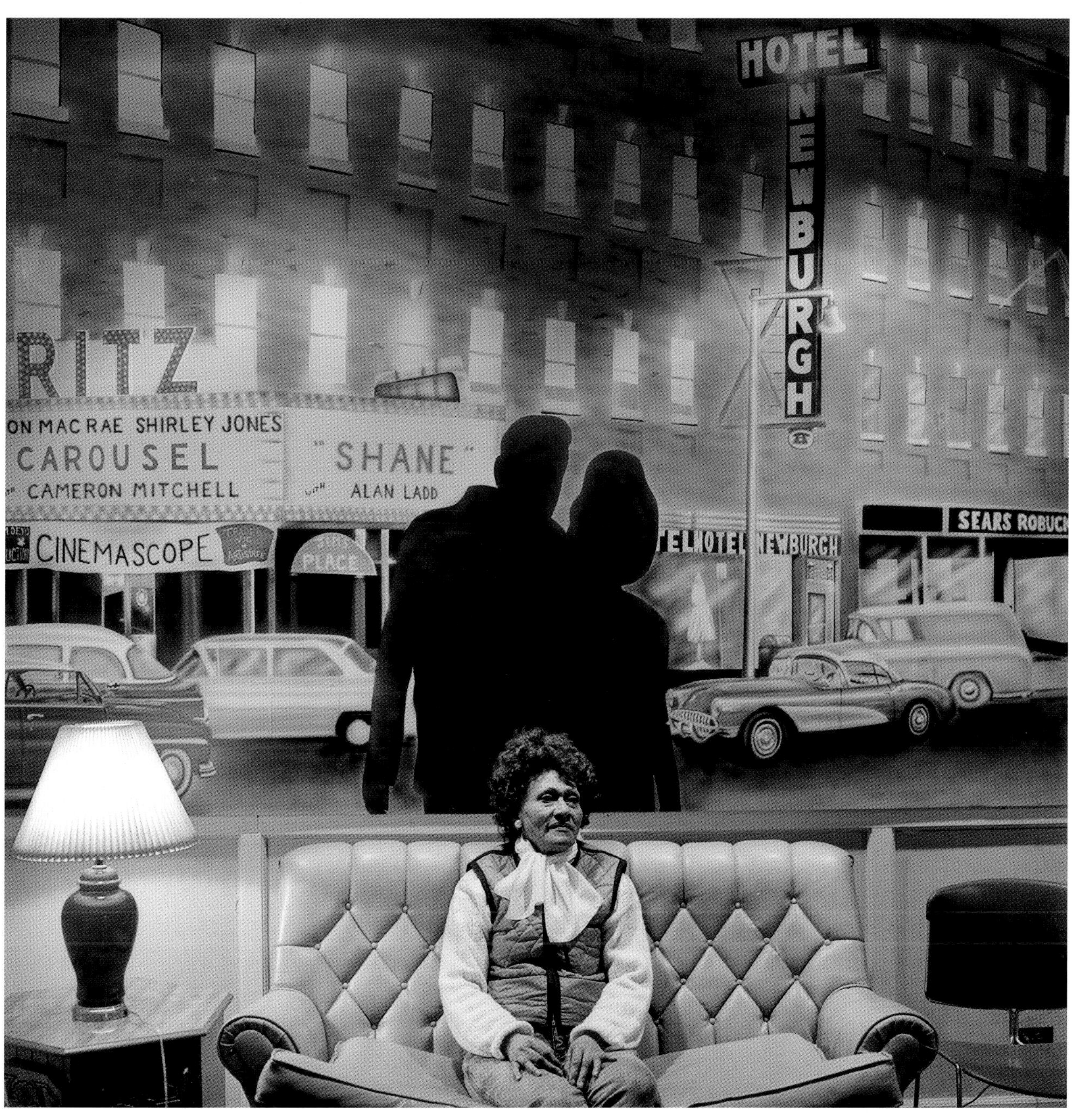
HOTEL
NEWBURGH
RITZ
SHIRLEY JONES
CAROUSEL
CAMERON MITCHELL
"SHANE"
WITH ALAN LADD
CINEMASCOPE
JIM'S PLACE
HOTEL NEWBURGH
SEARS ROBUCK

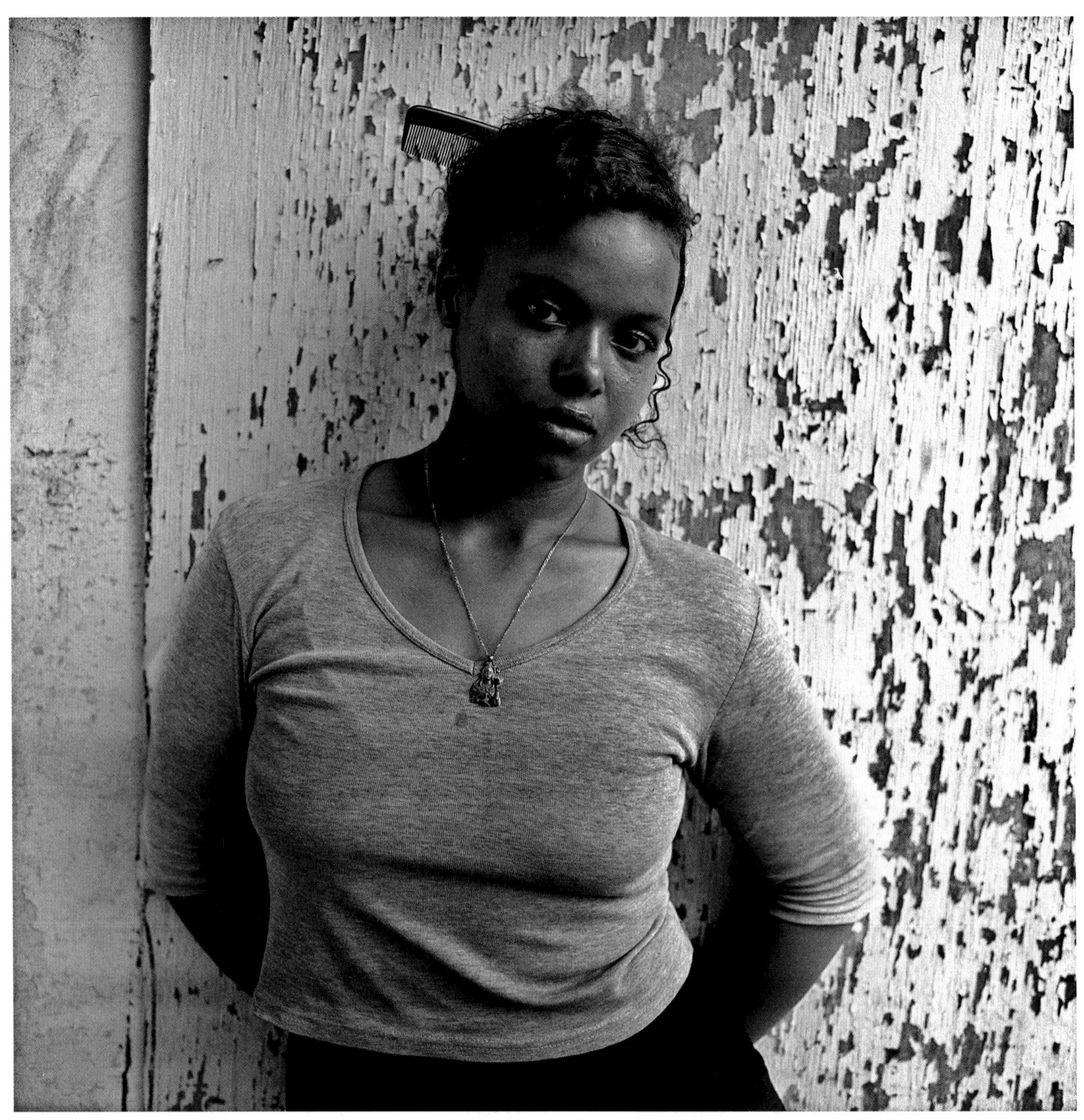

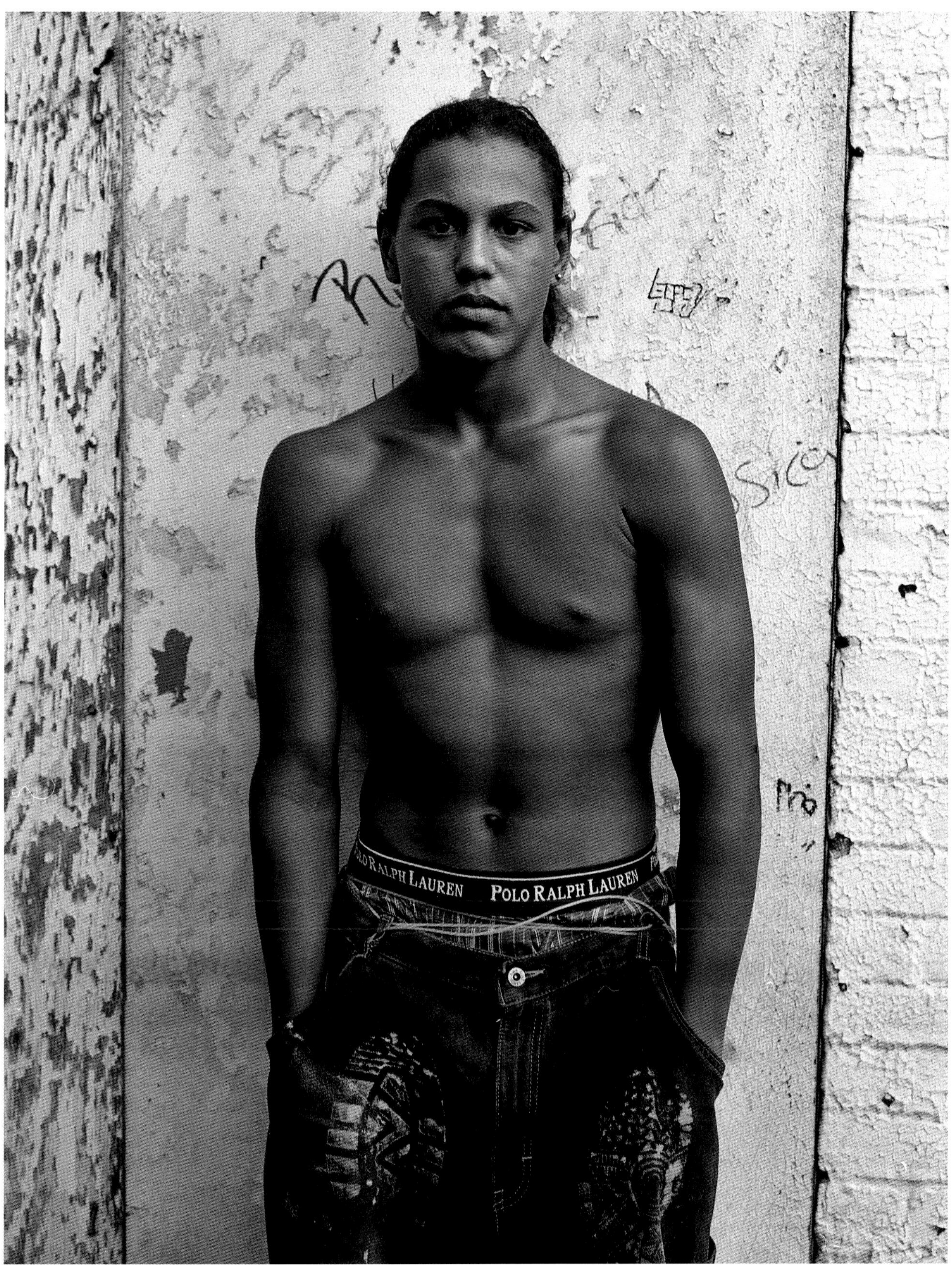
POLO RALPH LAUREN
POLO RALPH LAUREN

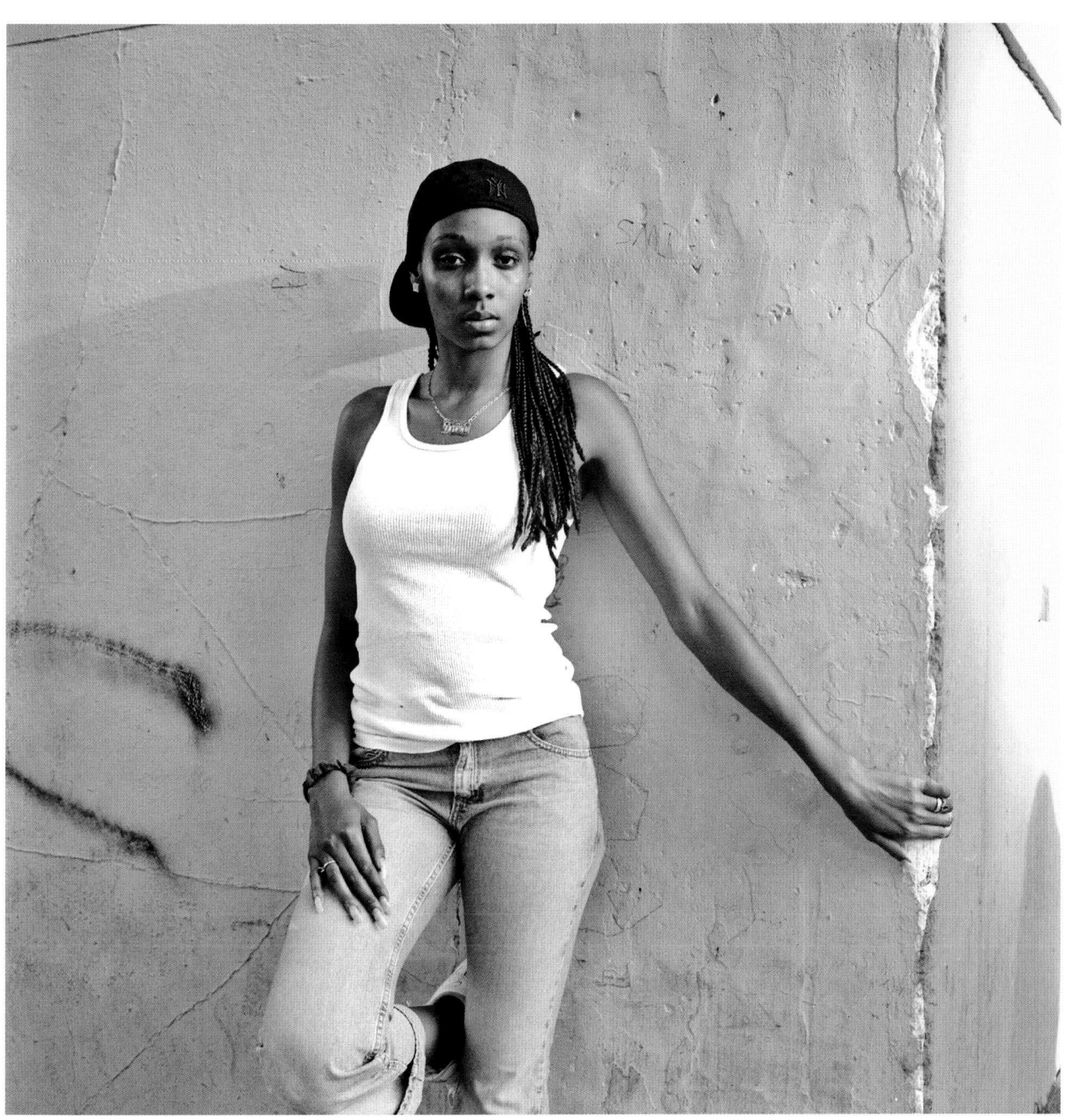

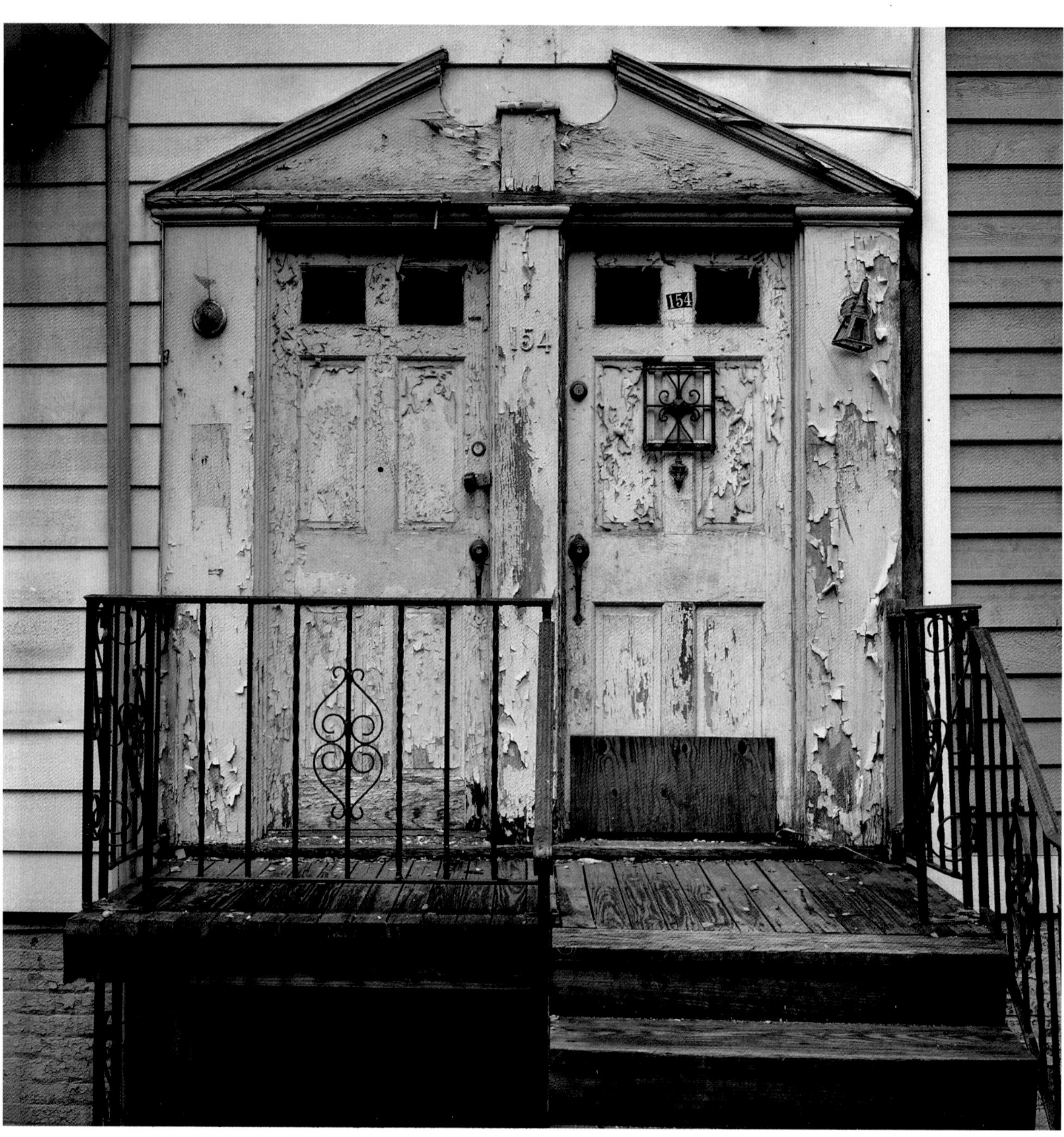
154
154

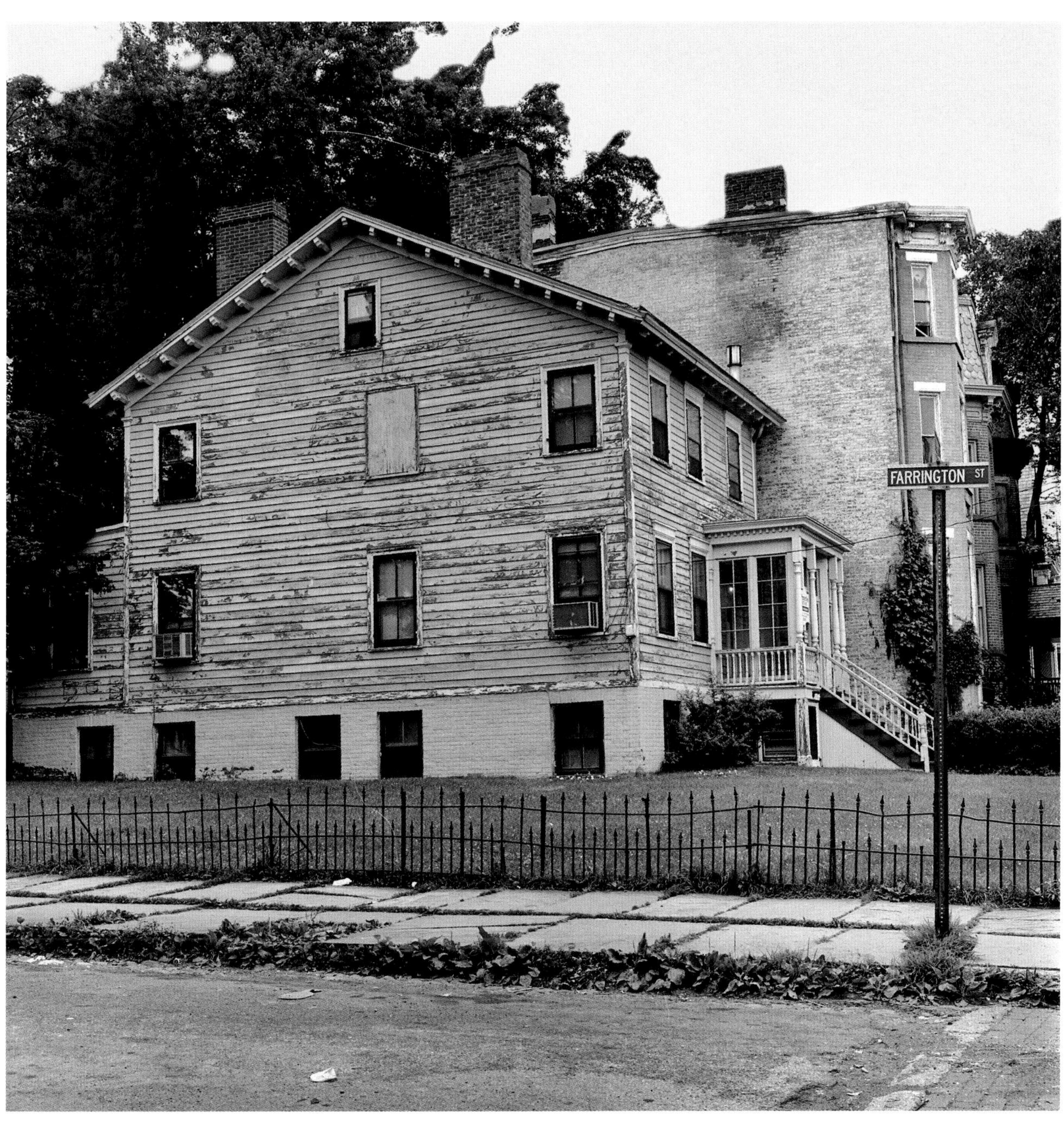
FARRINGTON ST

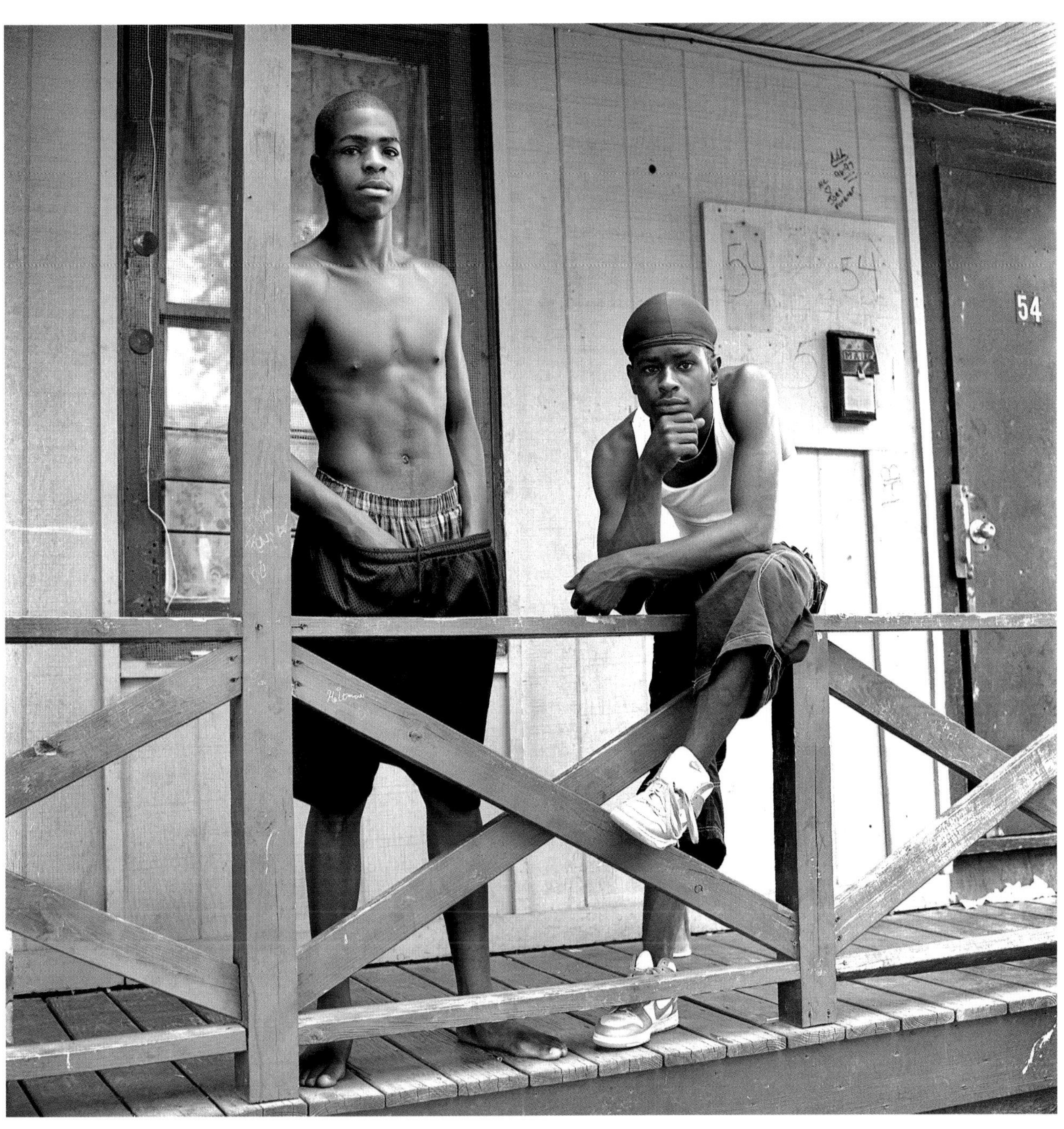
54

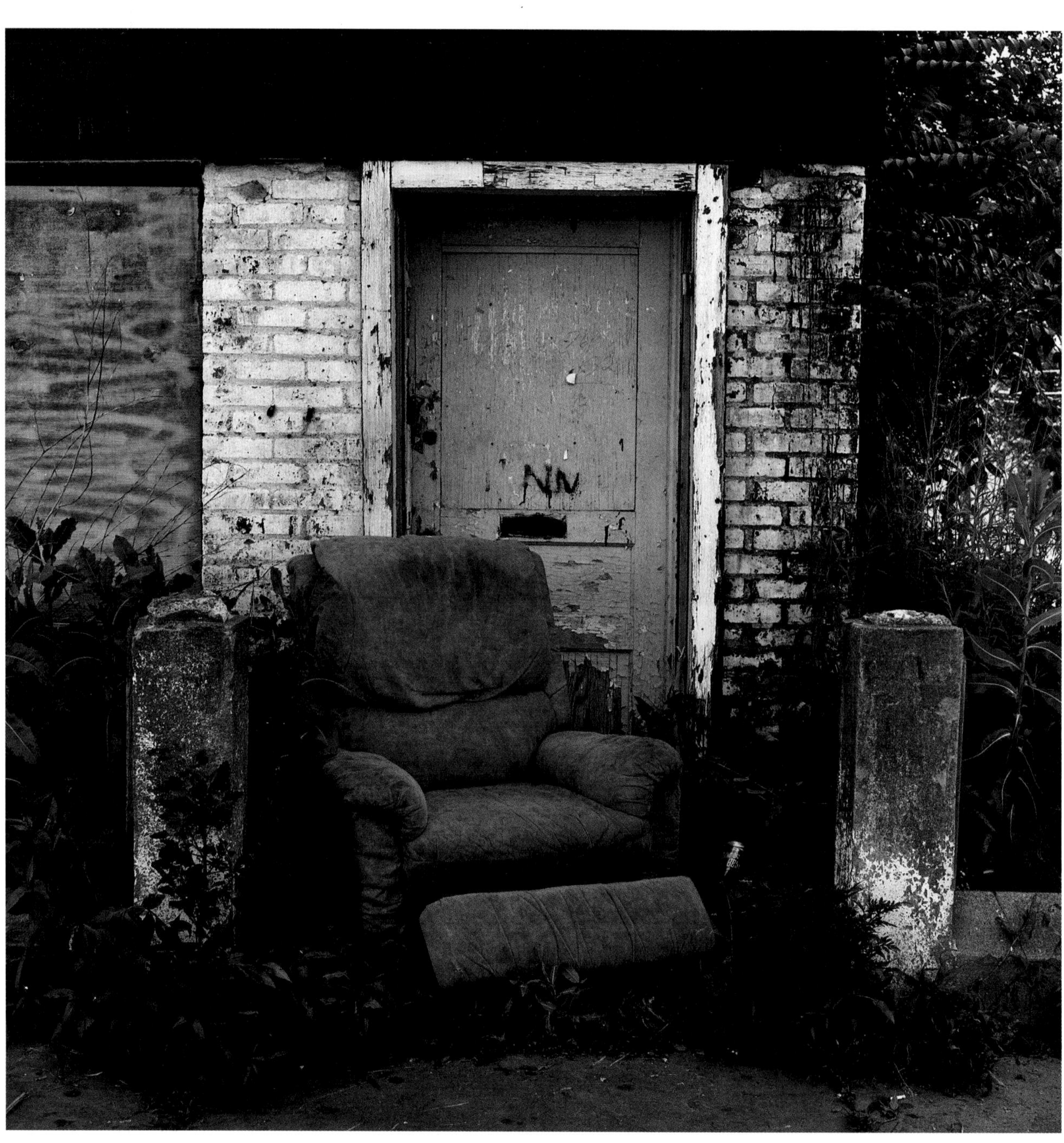

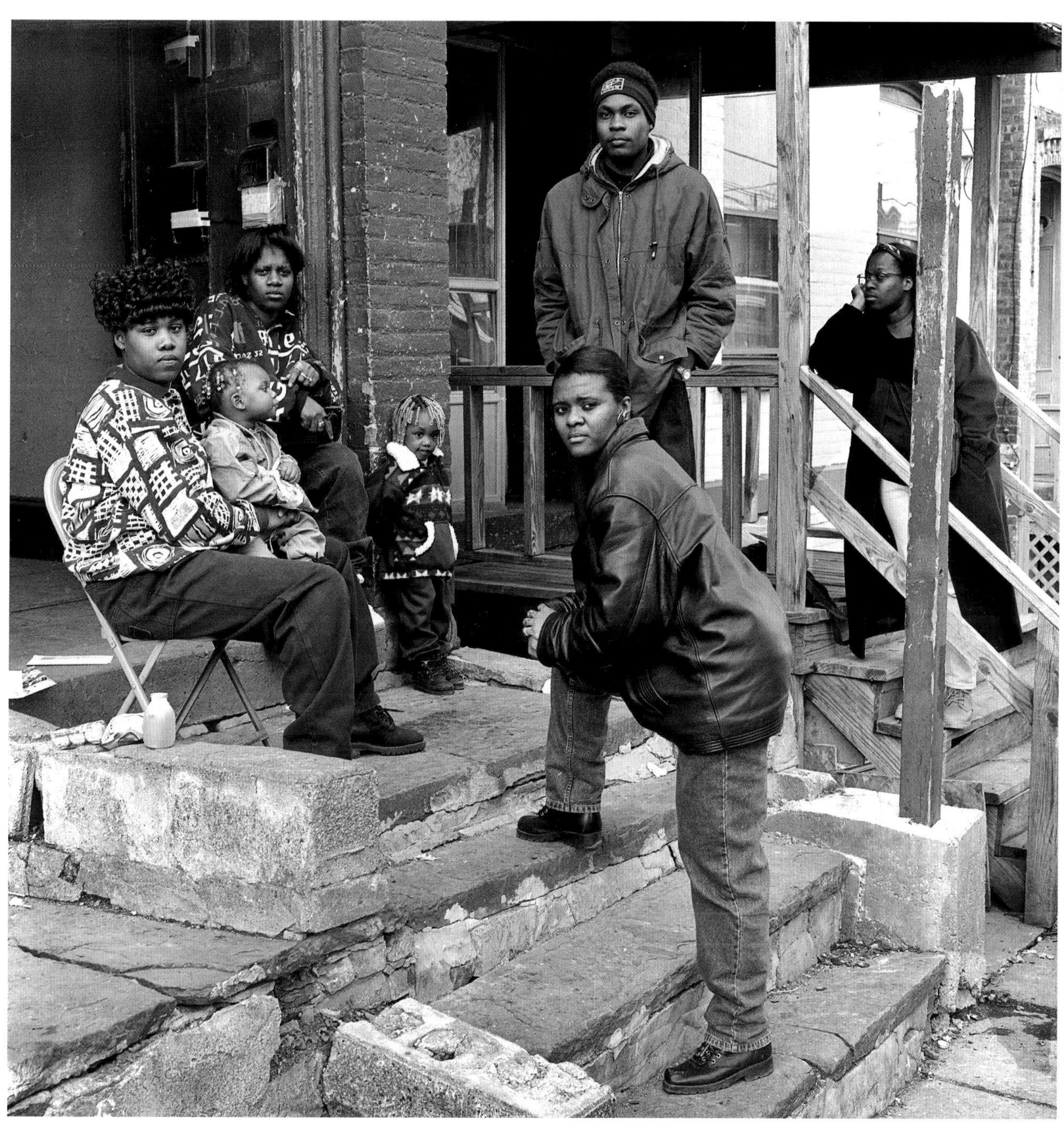

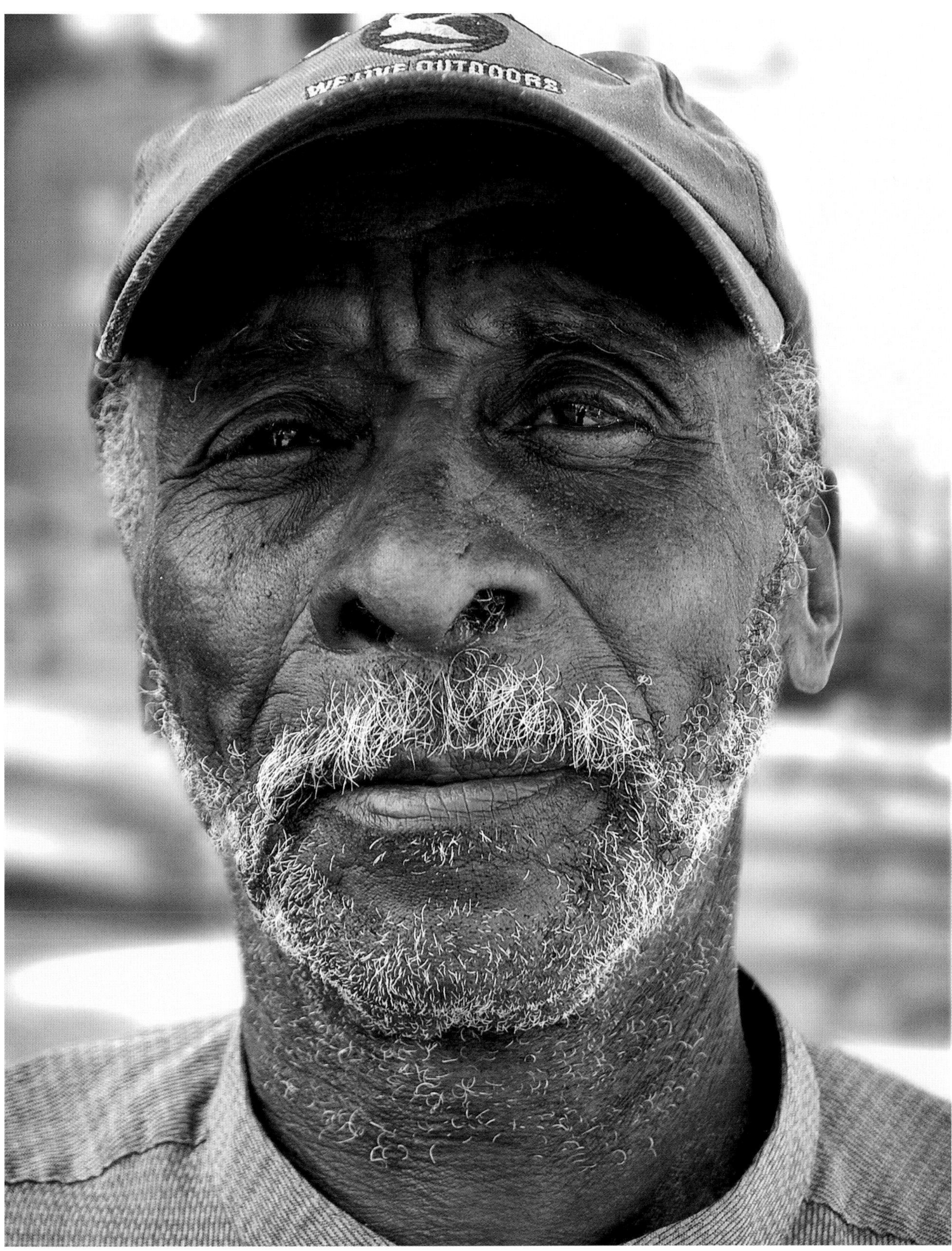
WE LIVE OUTDOORS

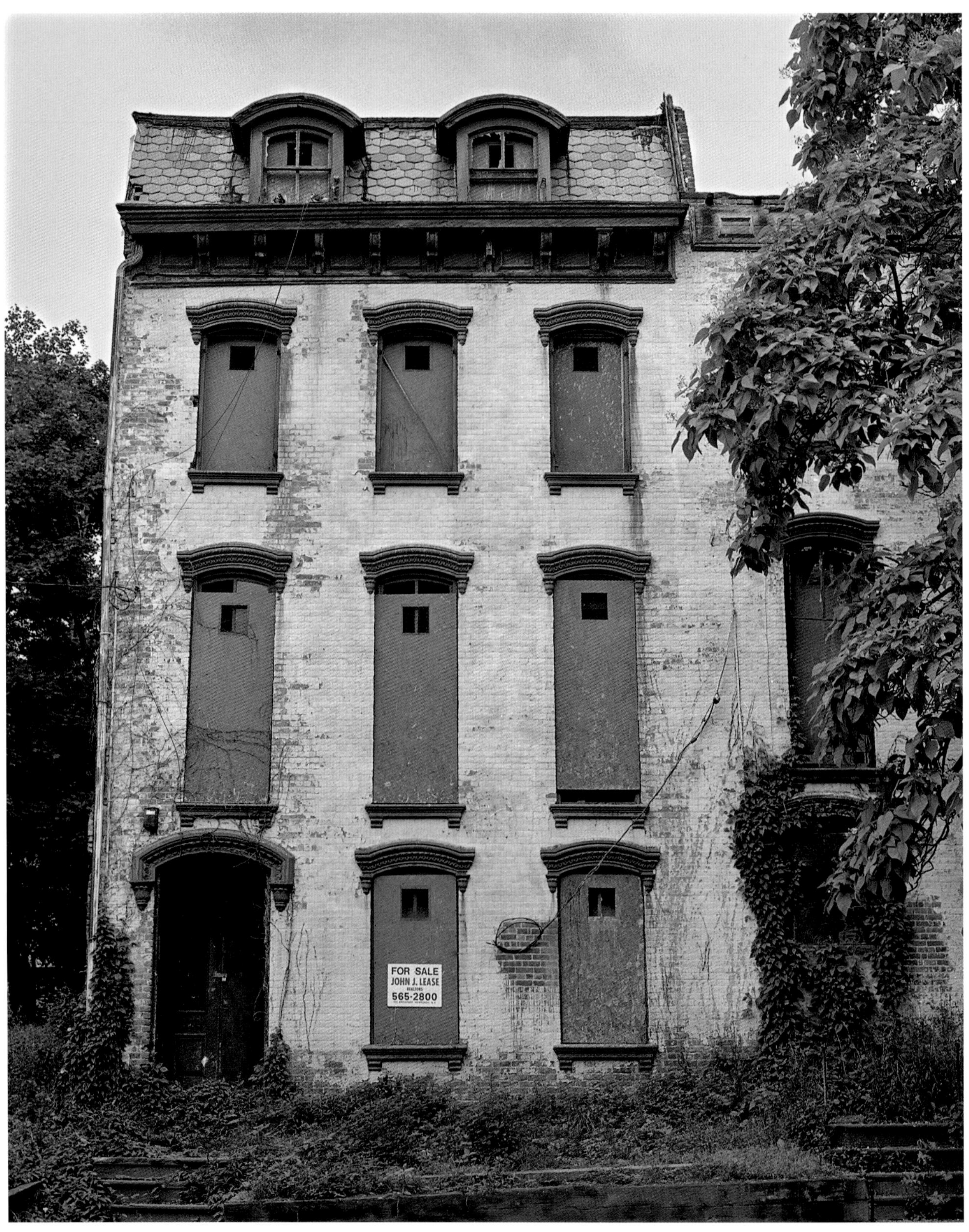
FOR SALE
JOHN J. LEASE
REALTORS
565-2800

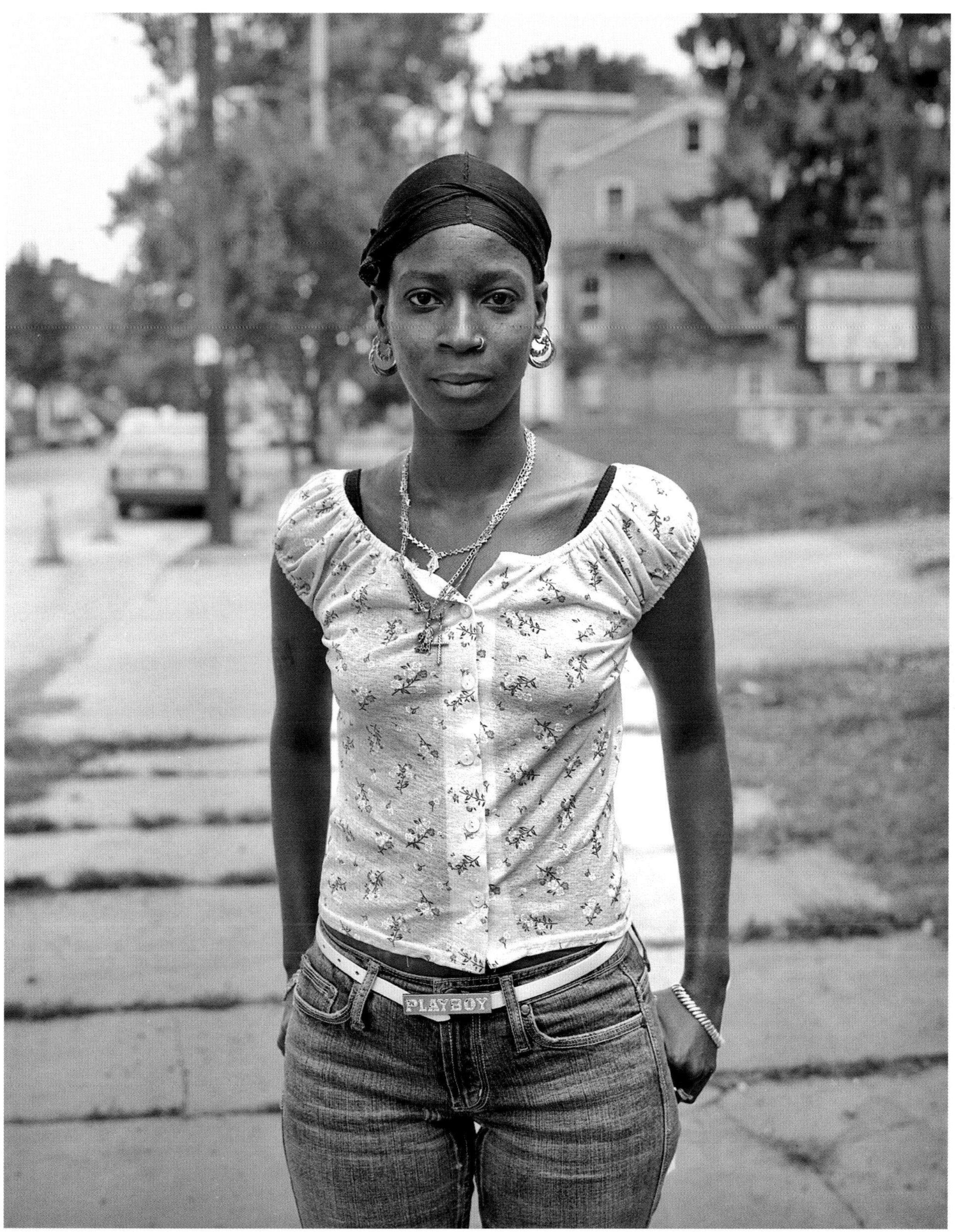
PLAYBOY

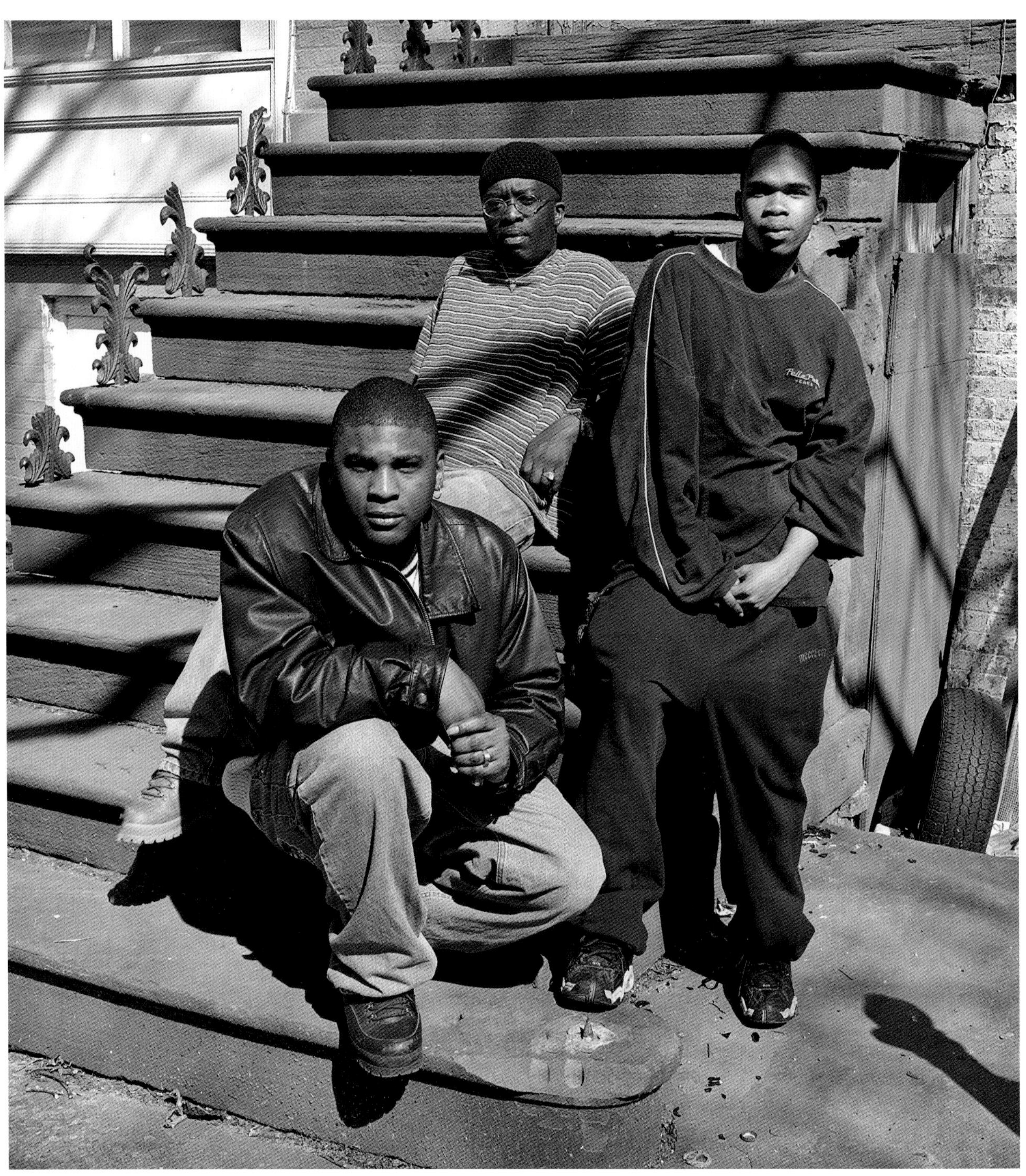

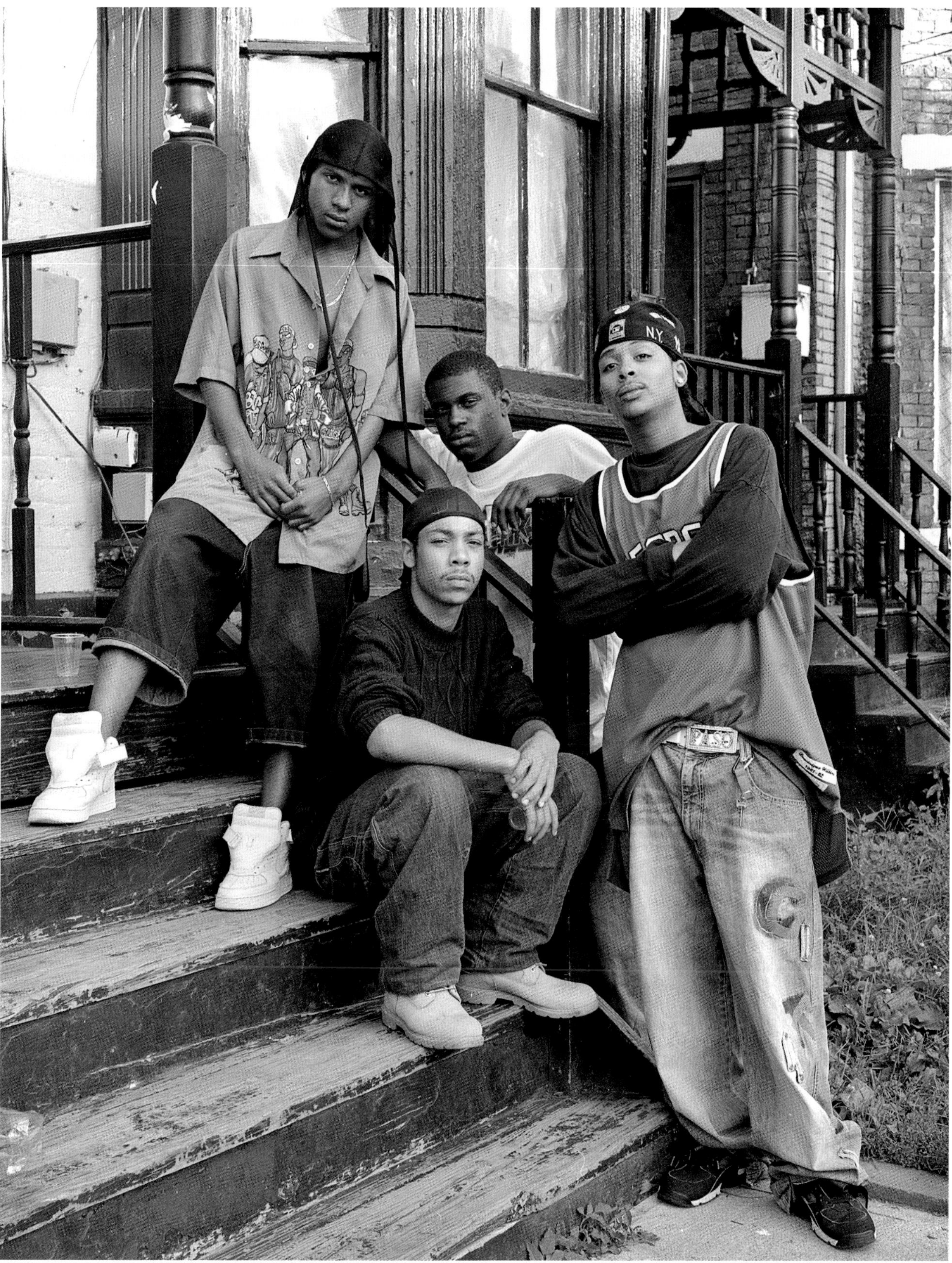

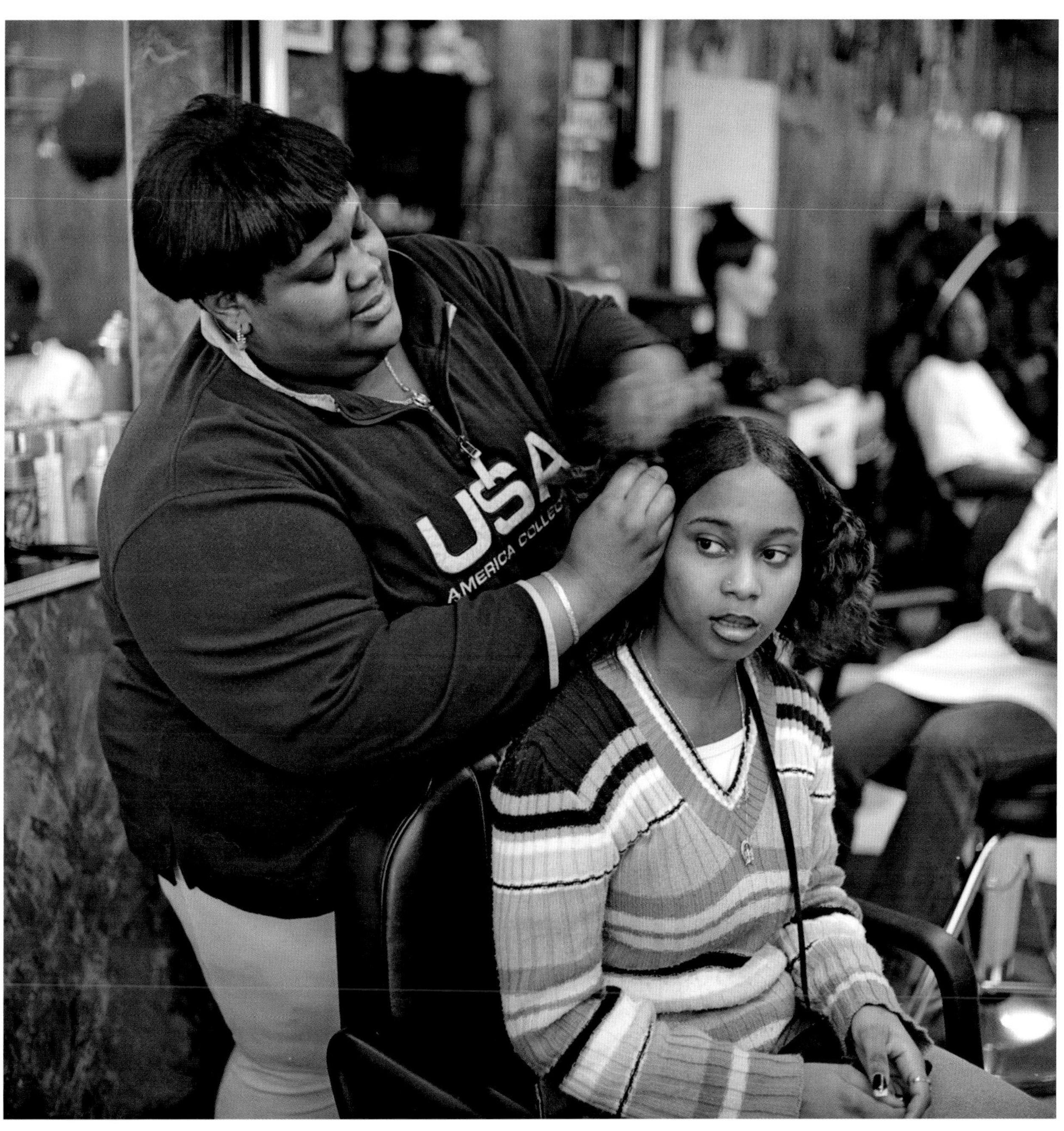
USA
AMERICA

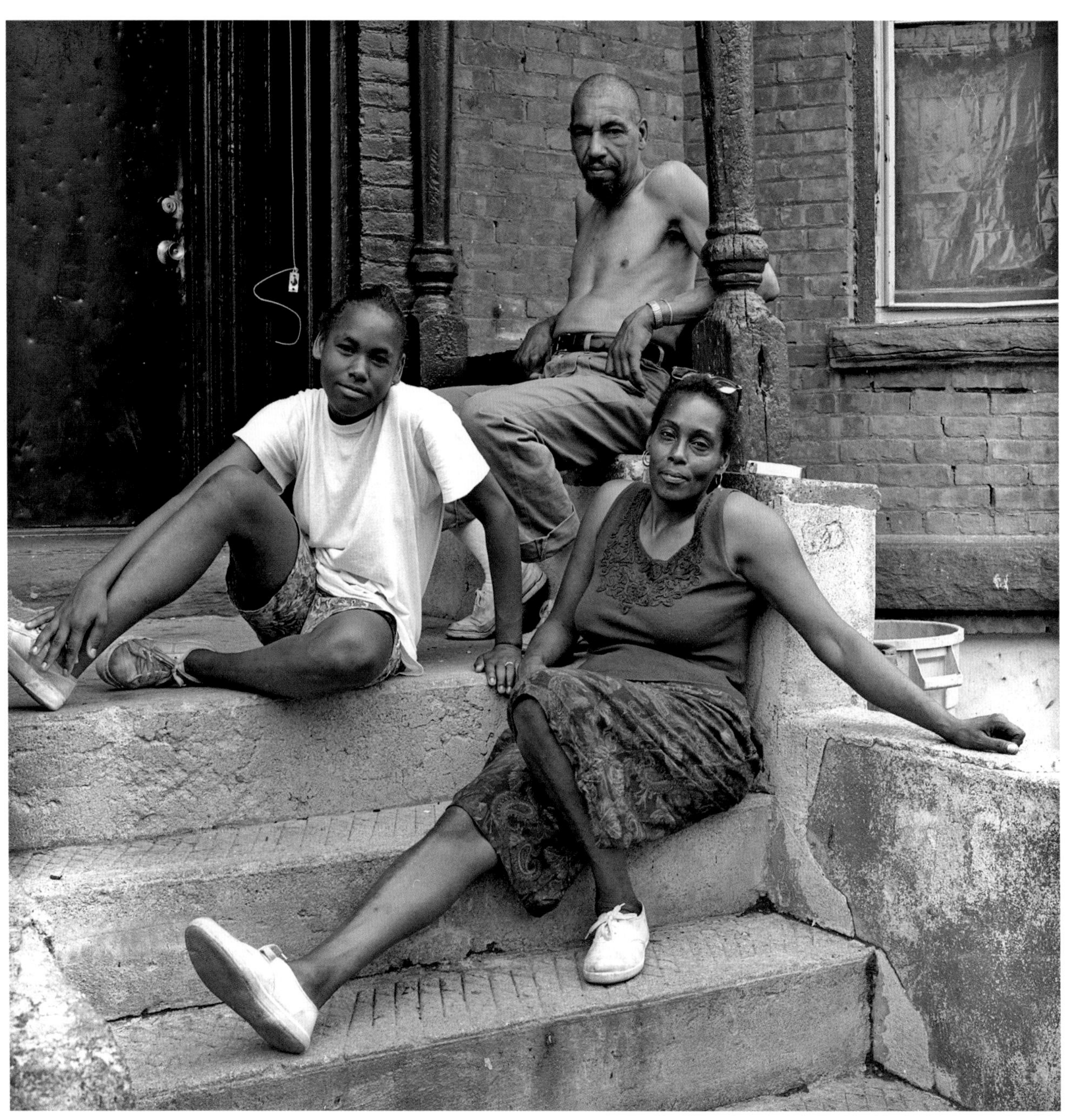

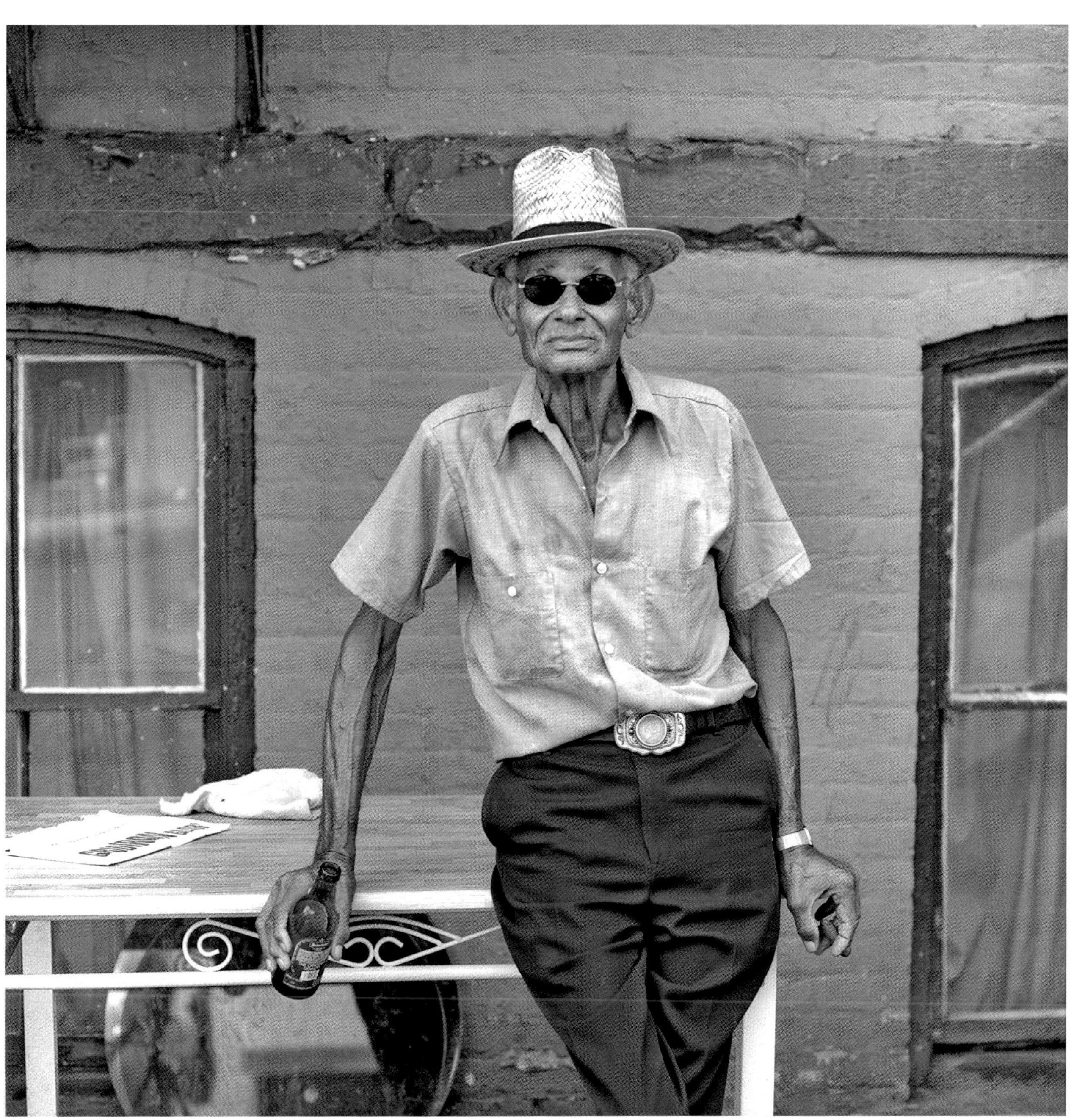

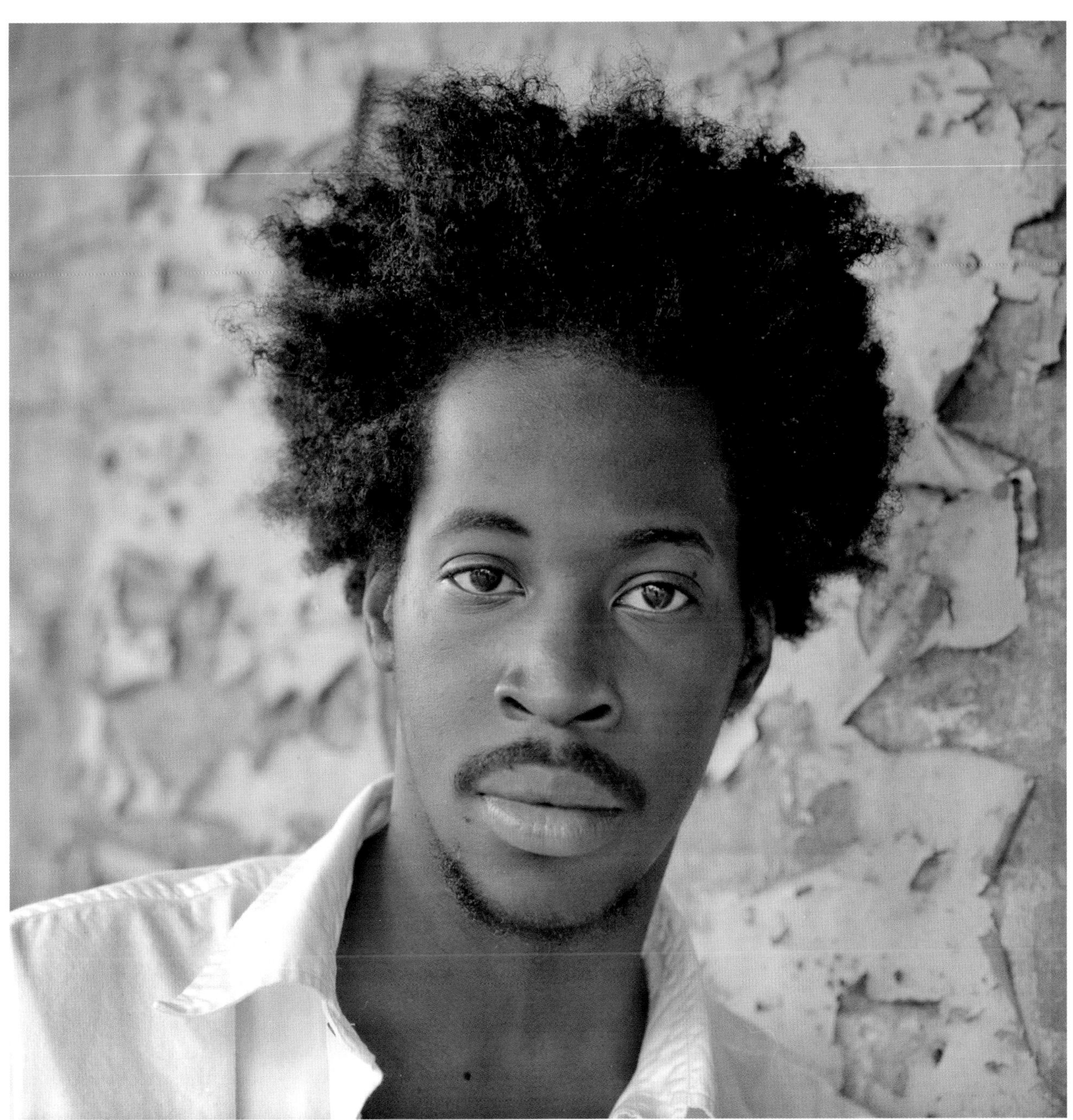

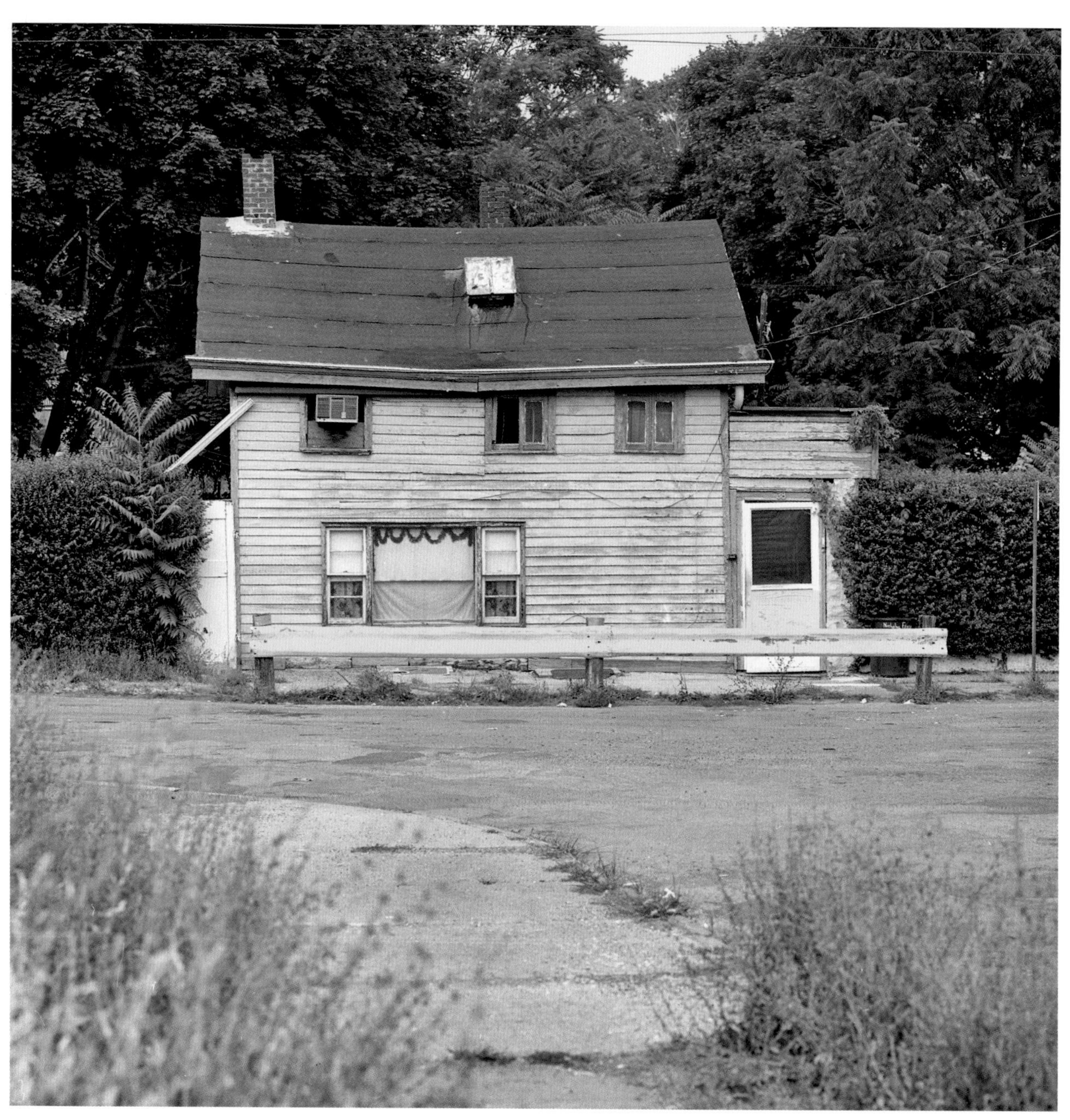

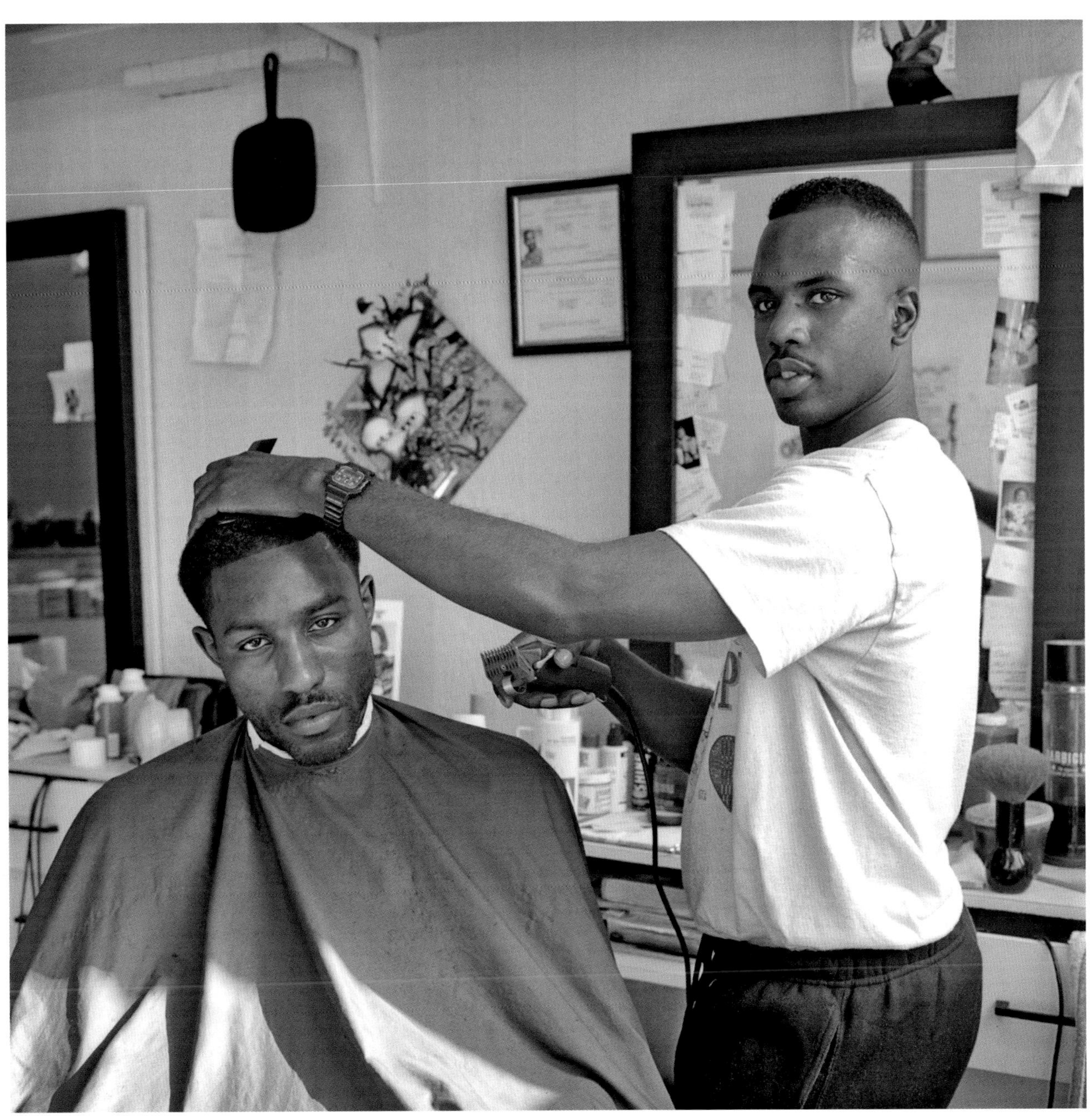

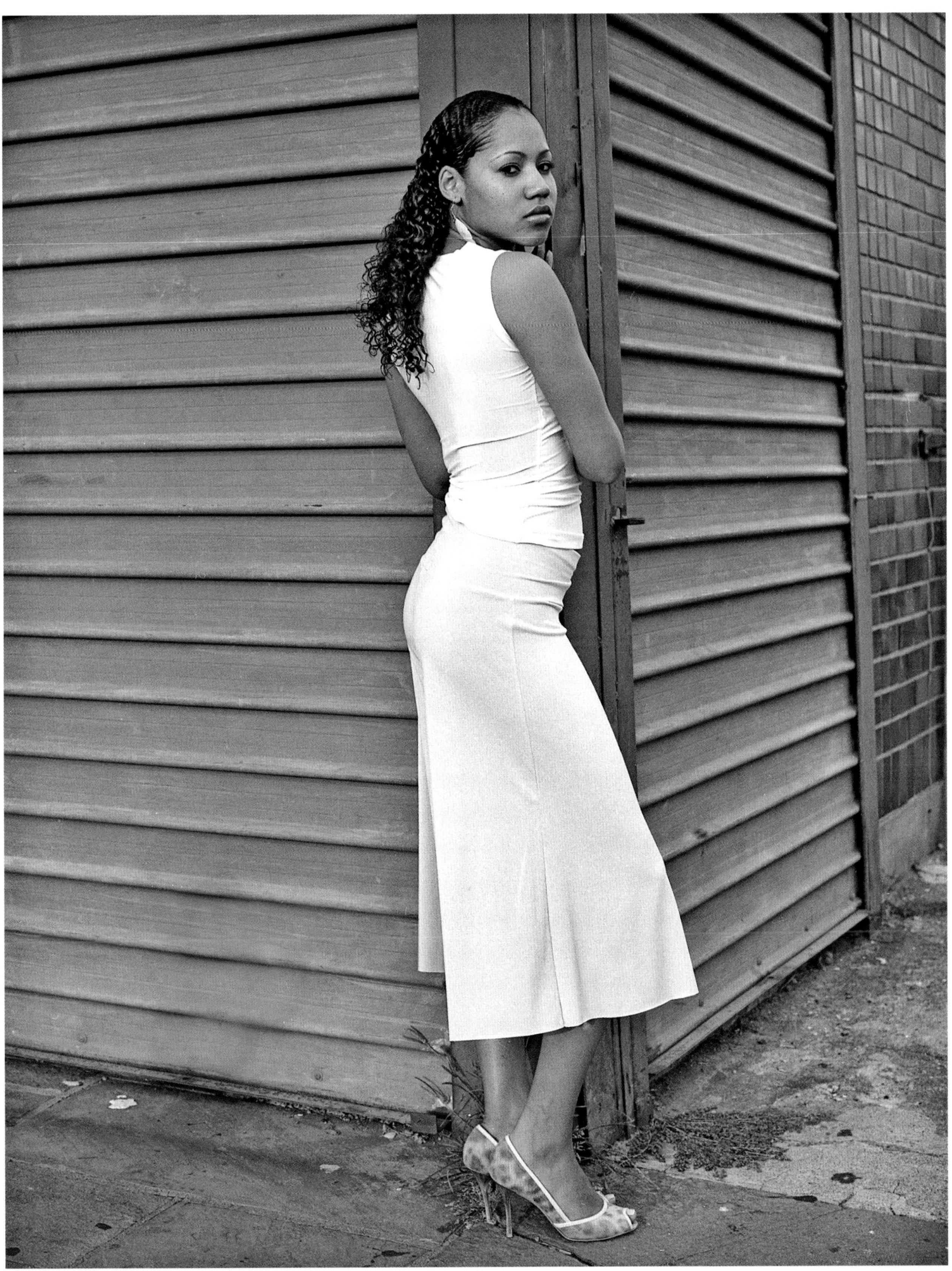

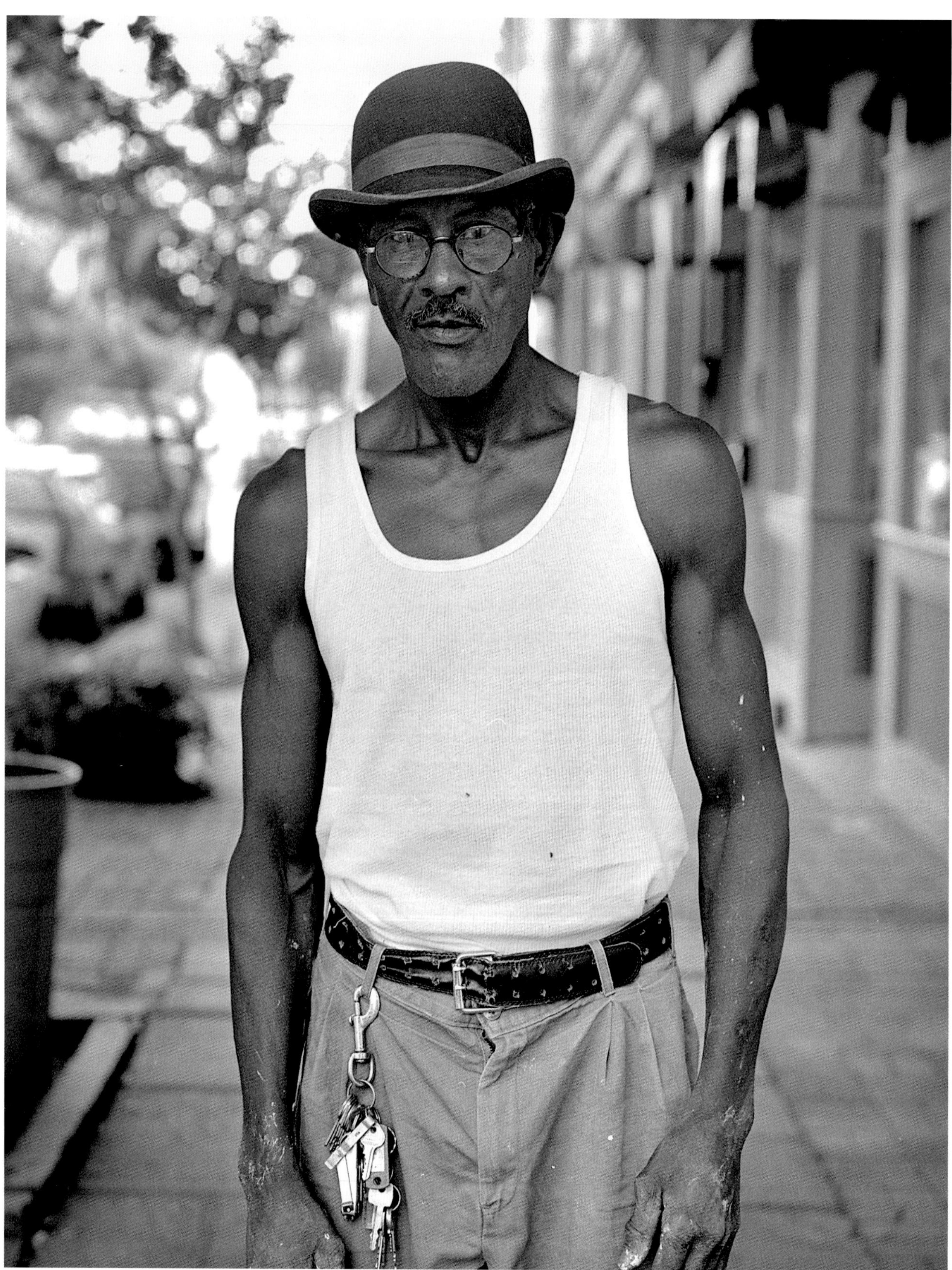

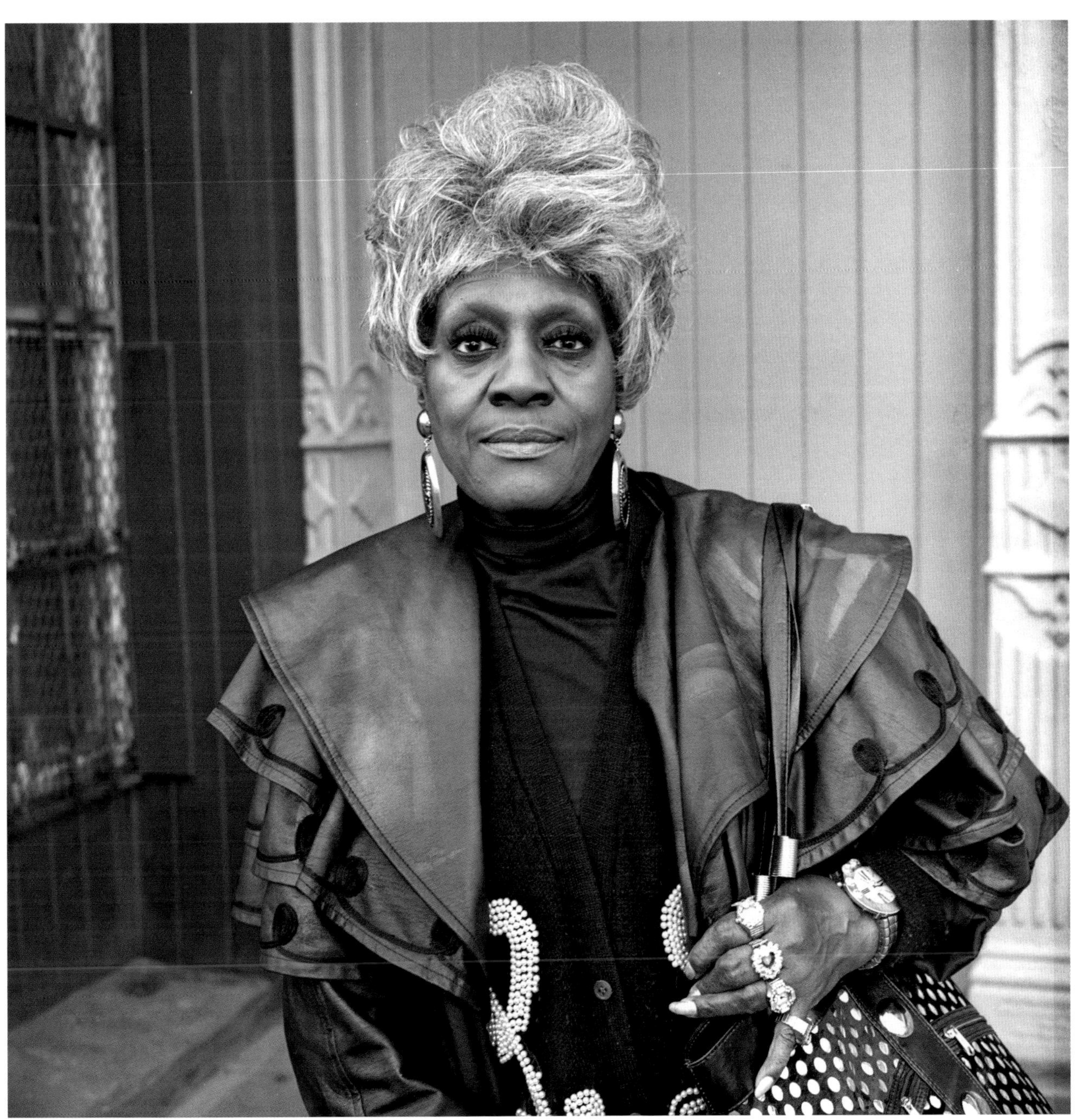

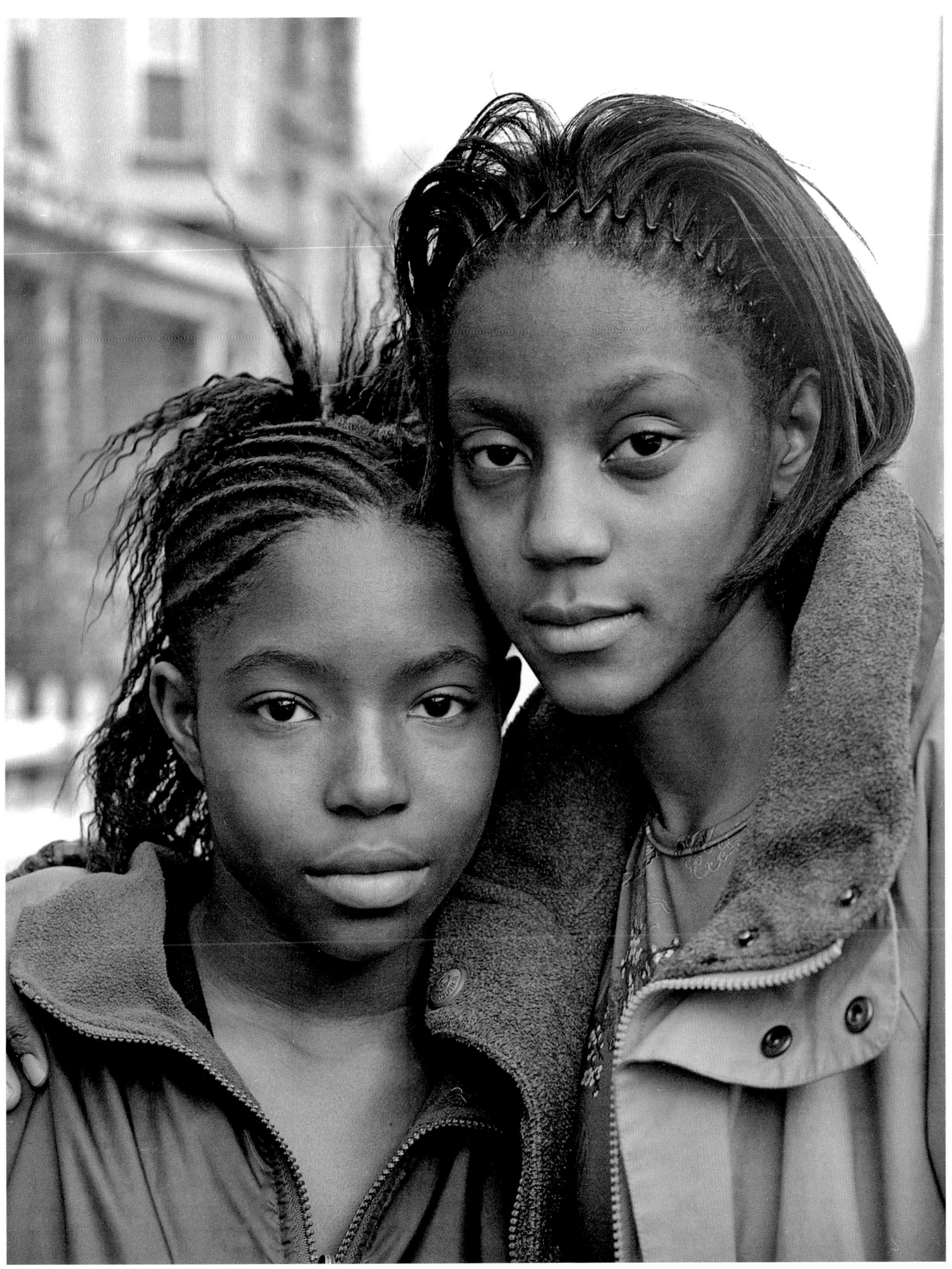

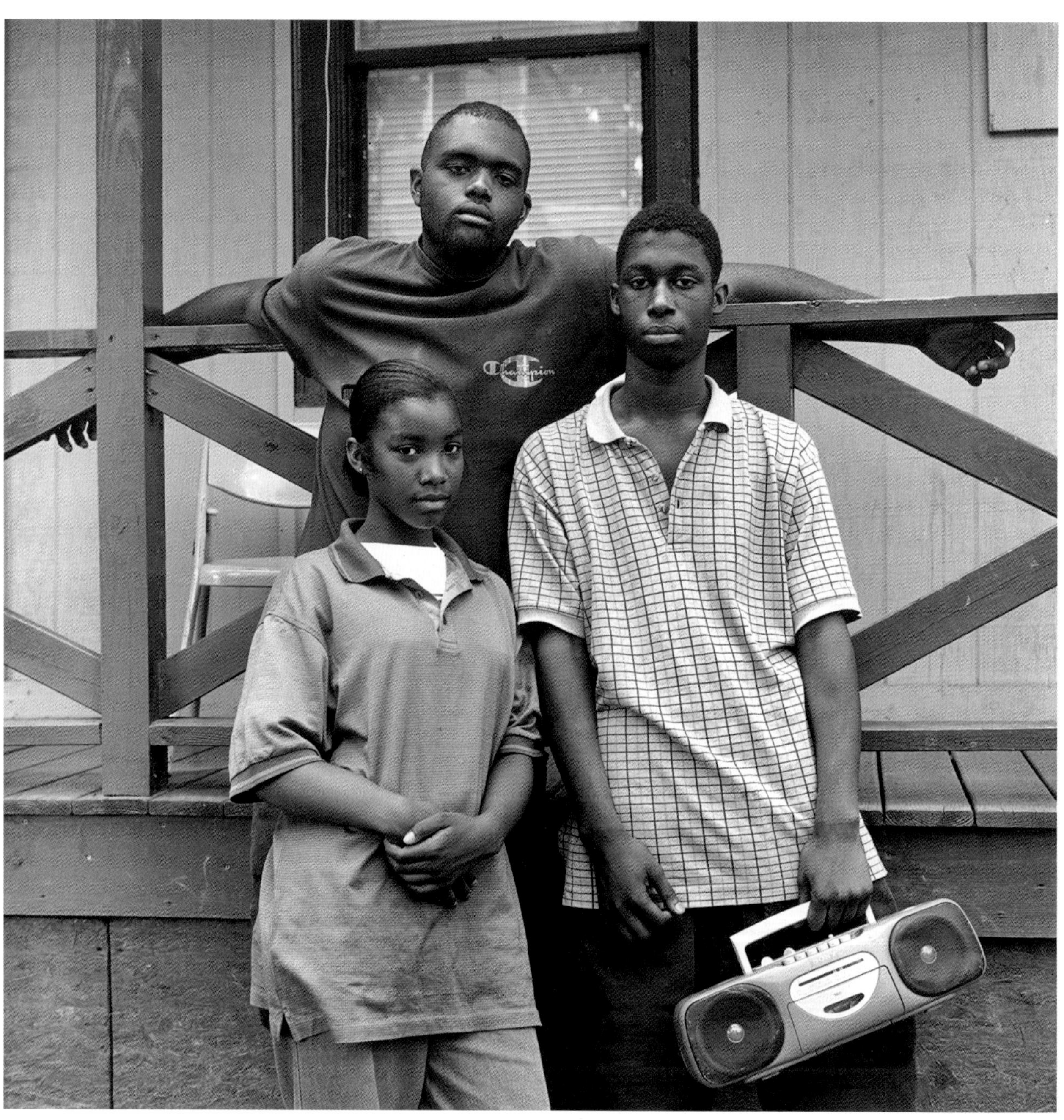
Champion

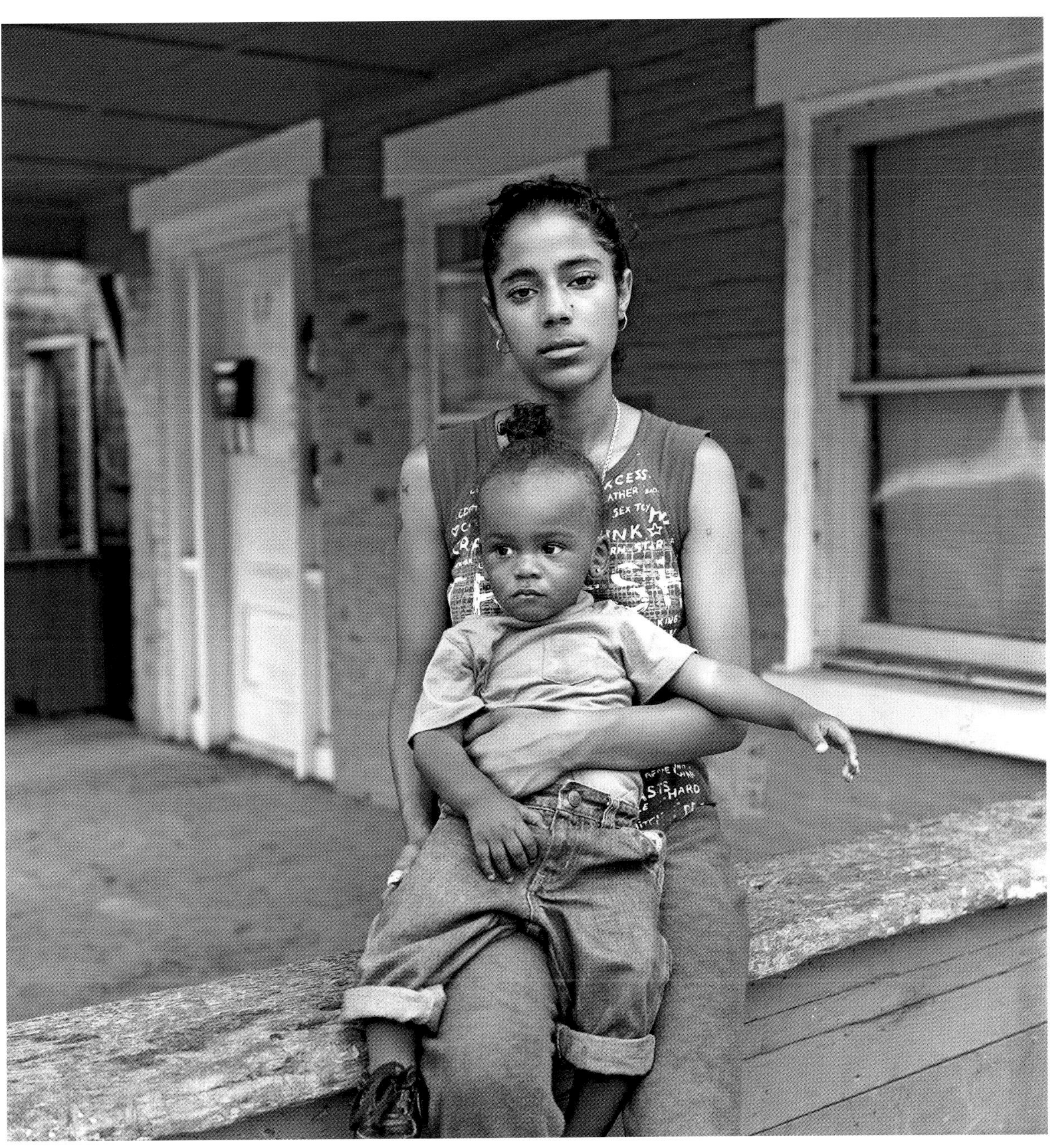

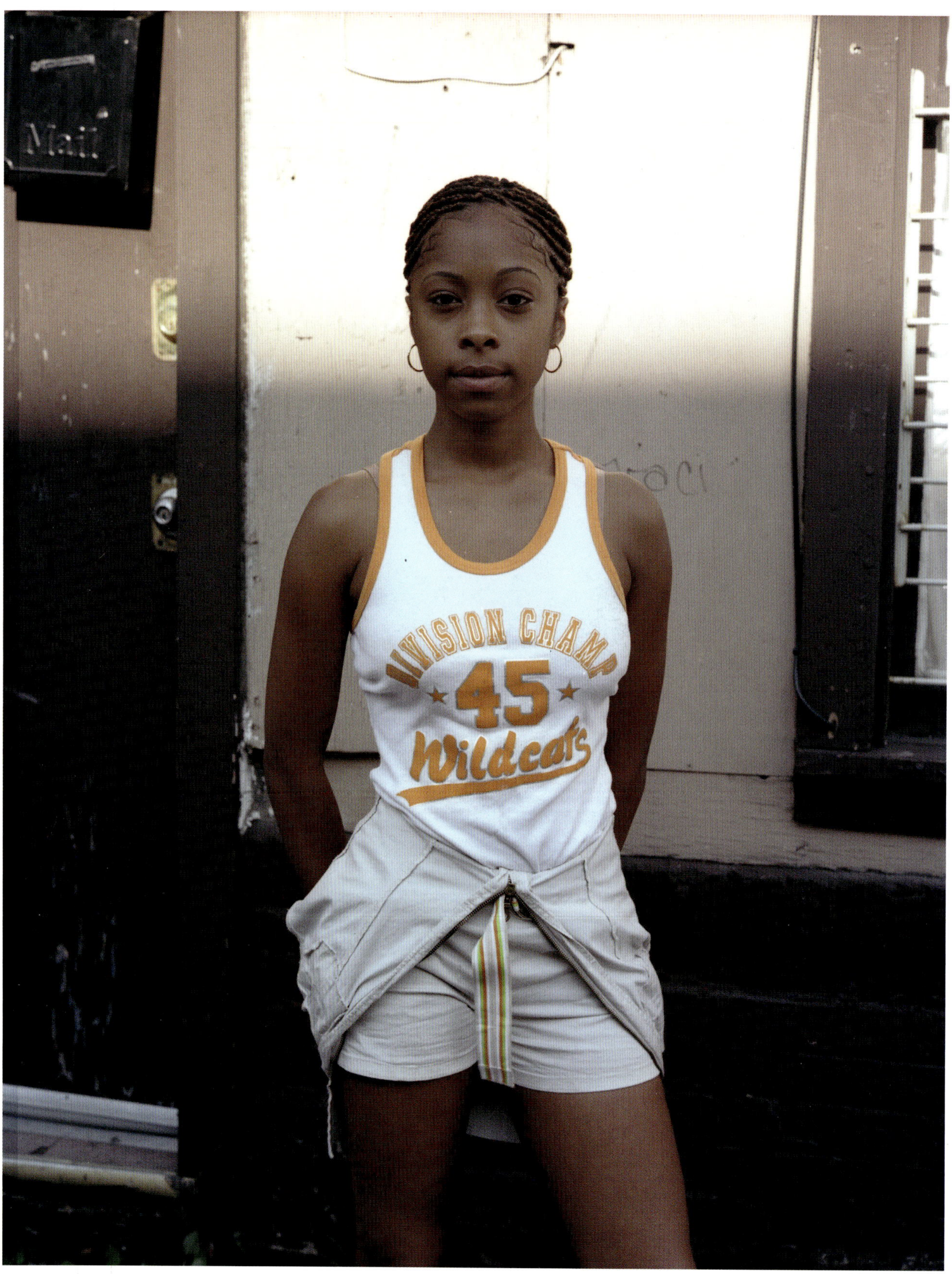
Mail
CHAMP
45
Wildcats

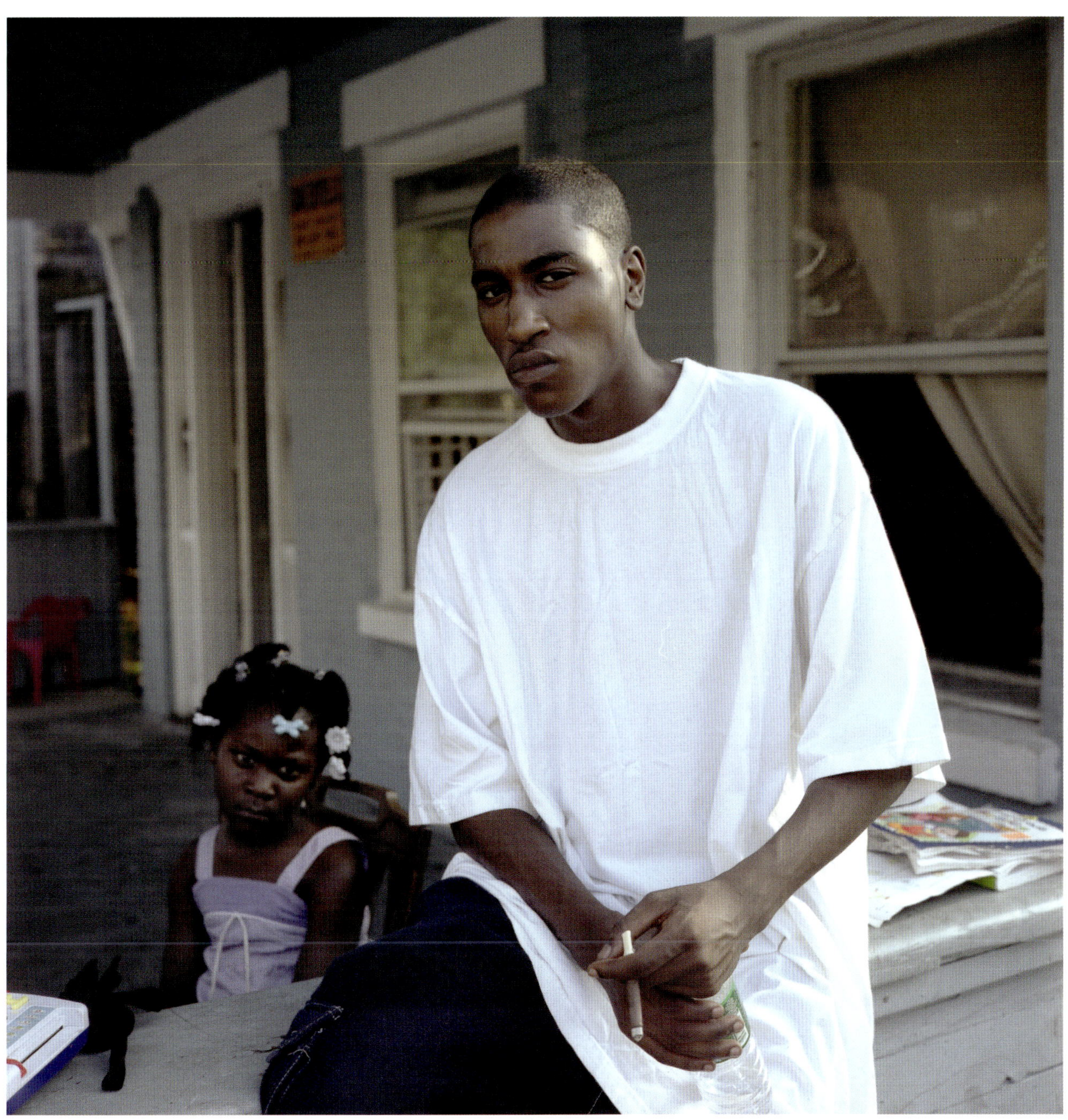

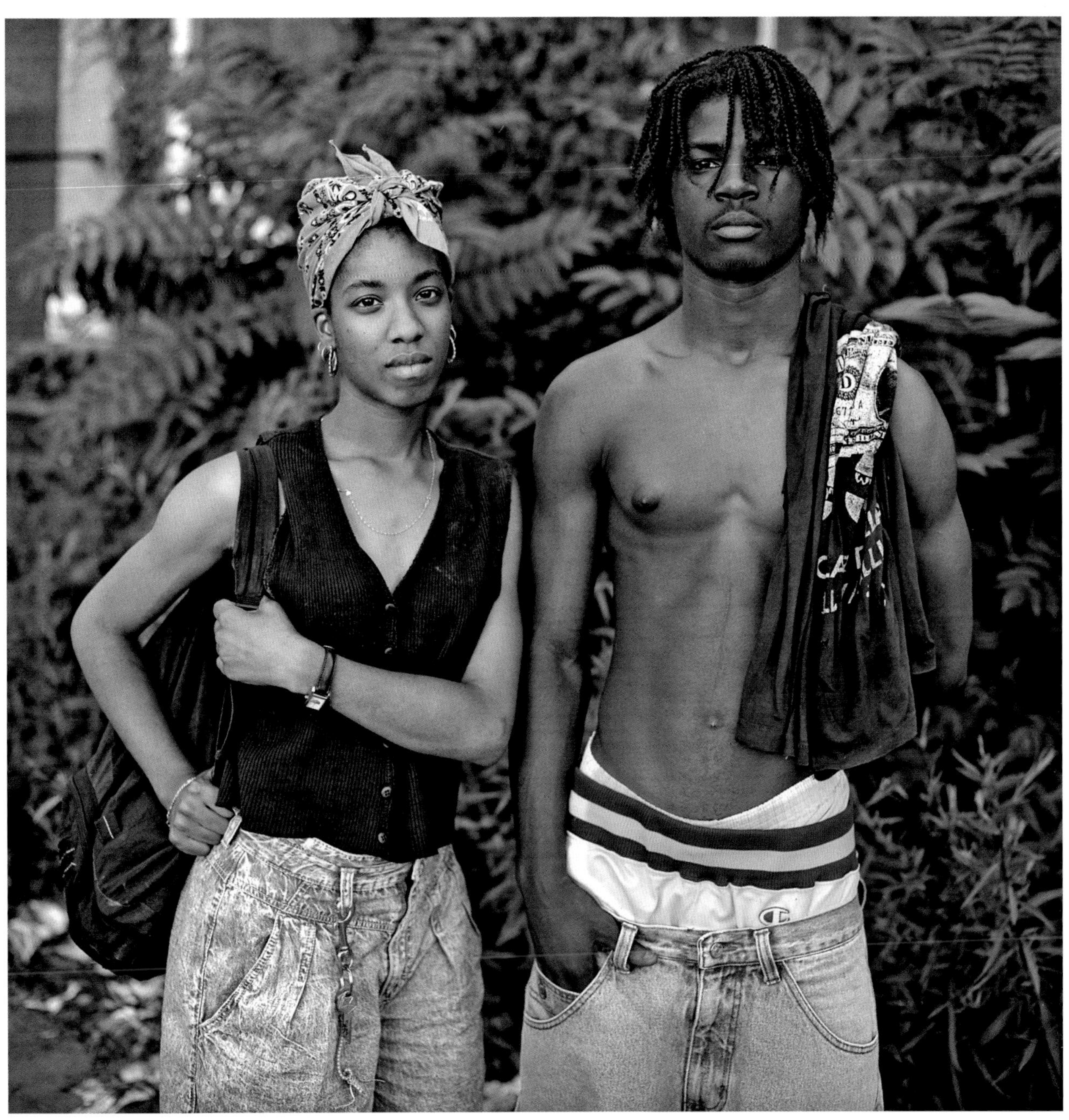

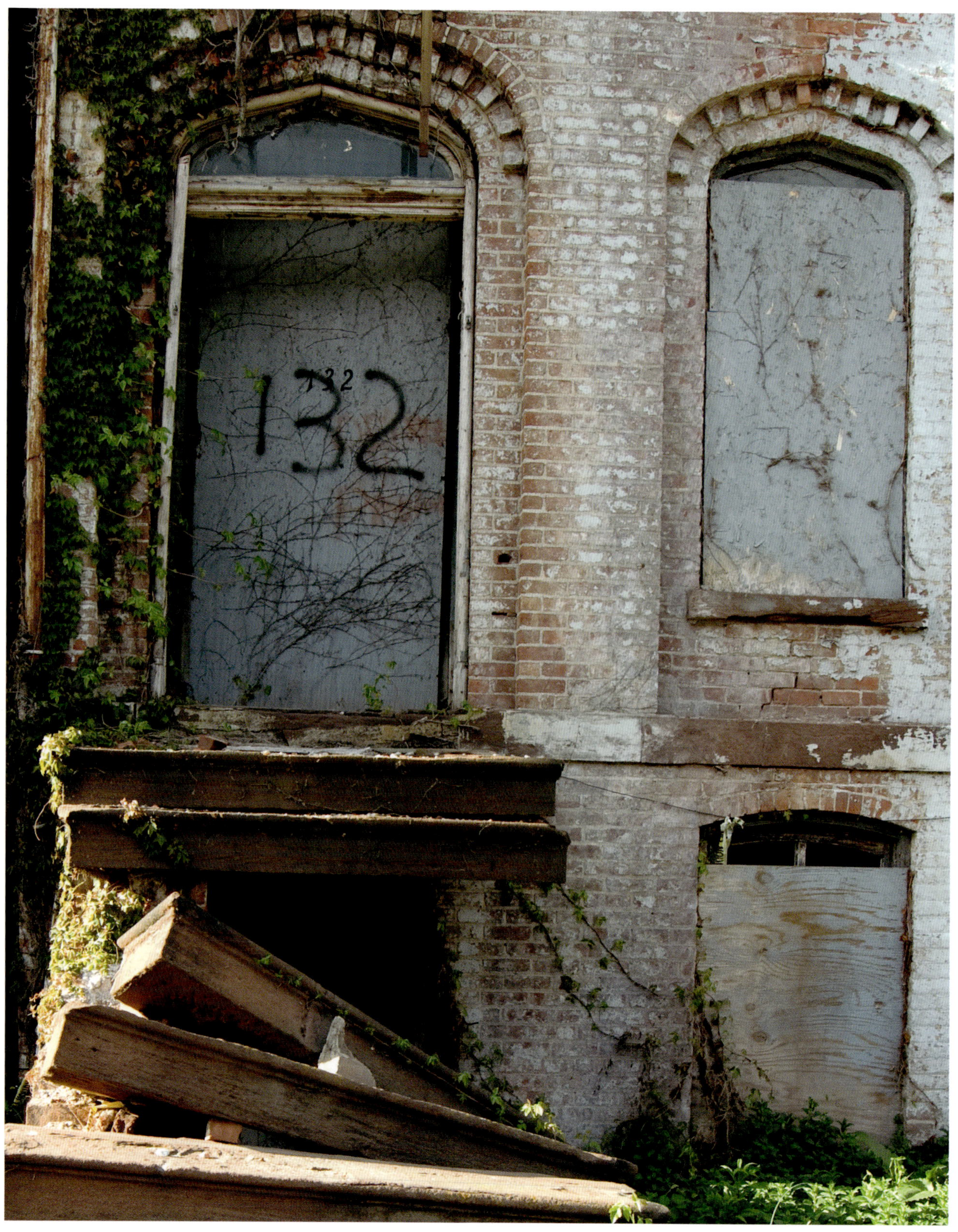
132
132

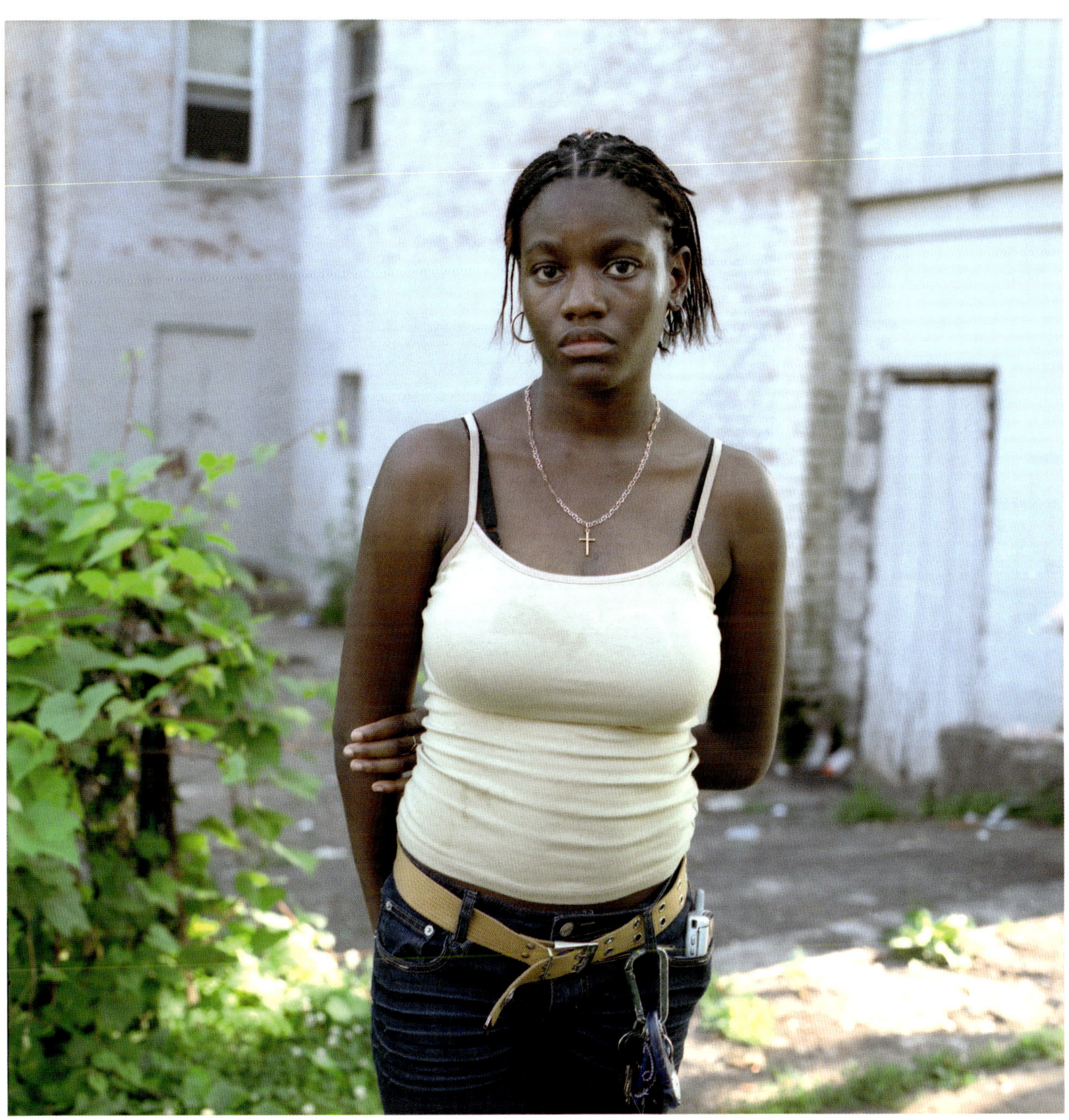

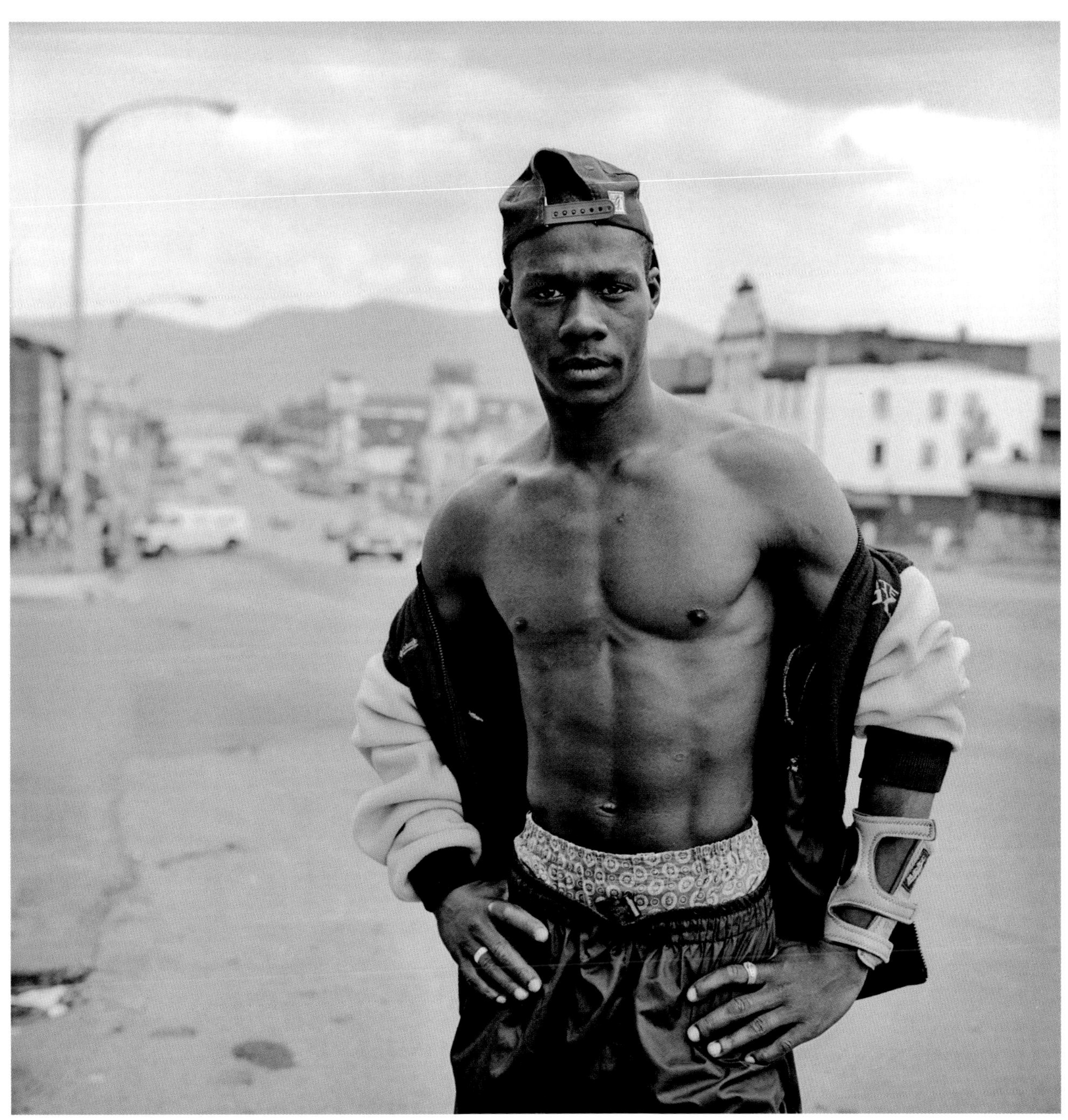

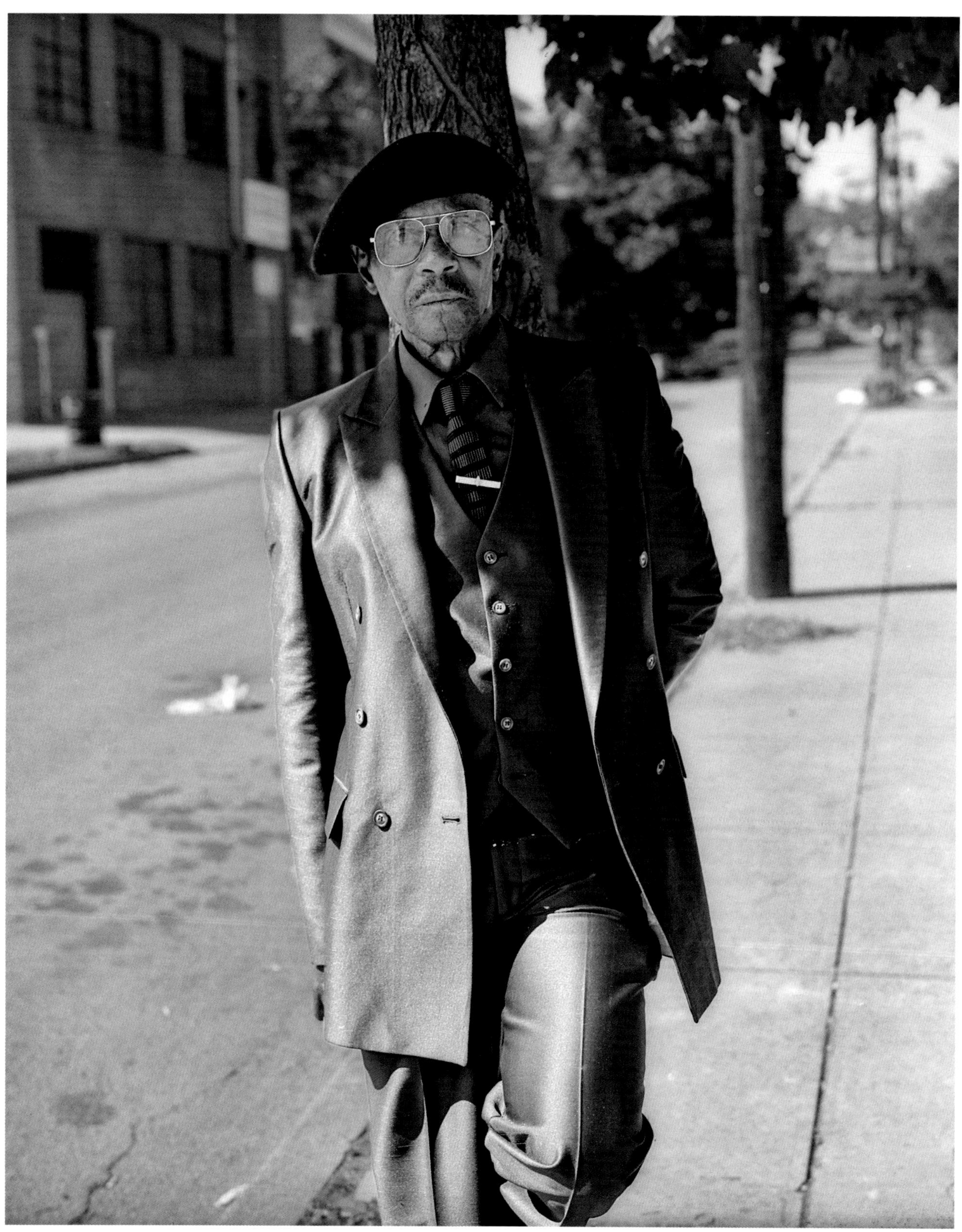

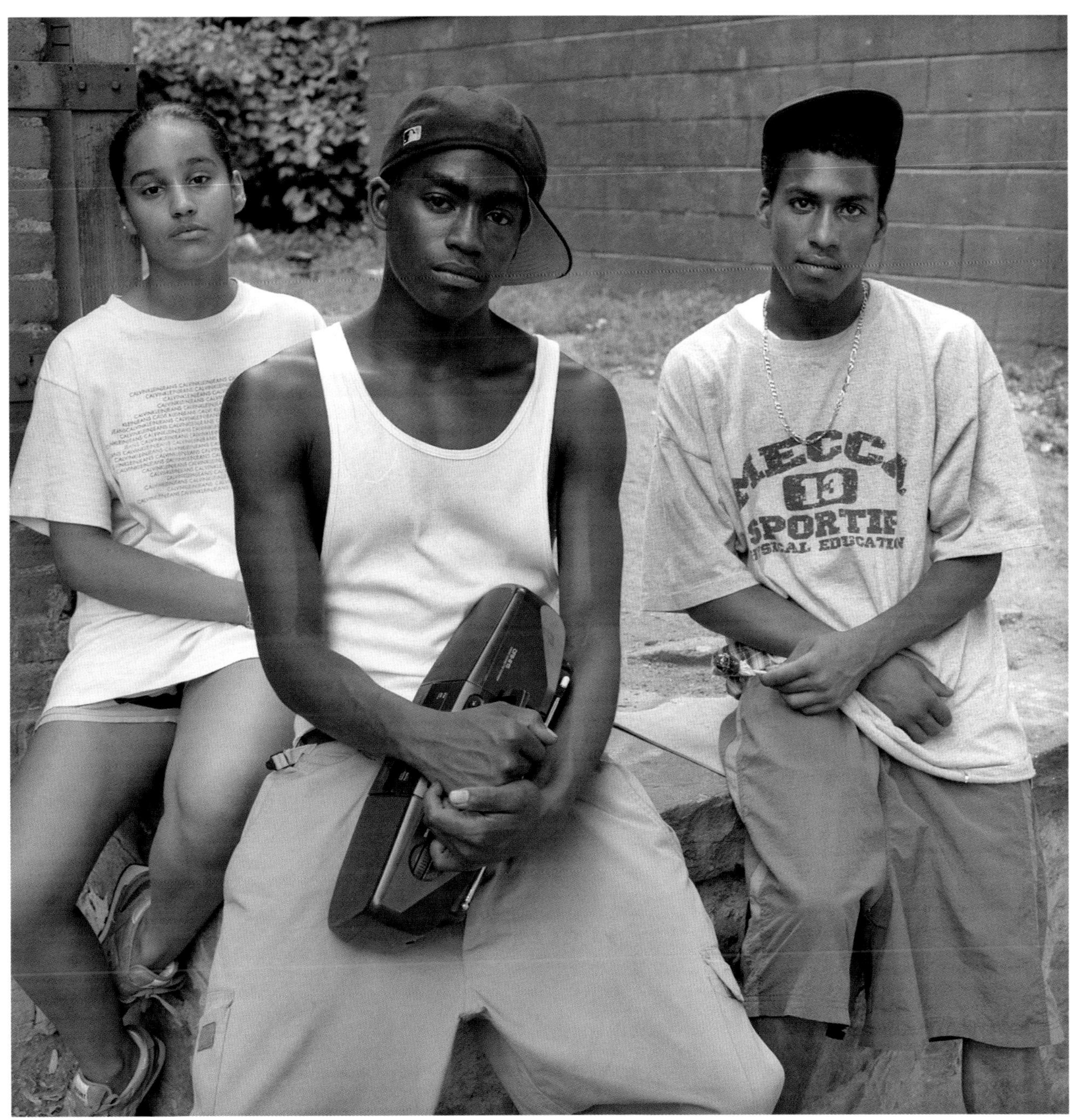
13
SPORTIF

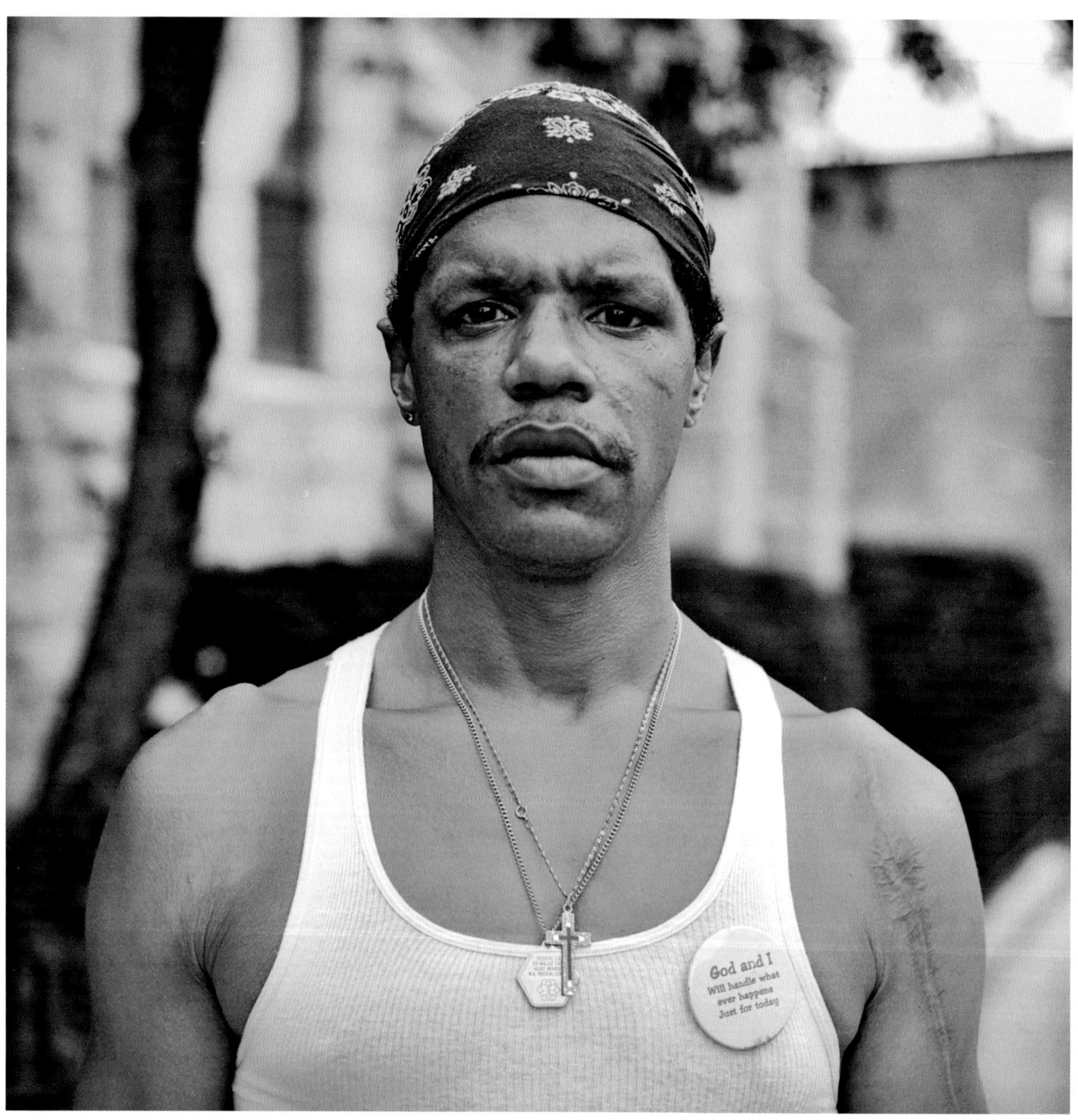
God and I
Will handle what
ever happens
Just for today

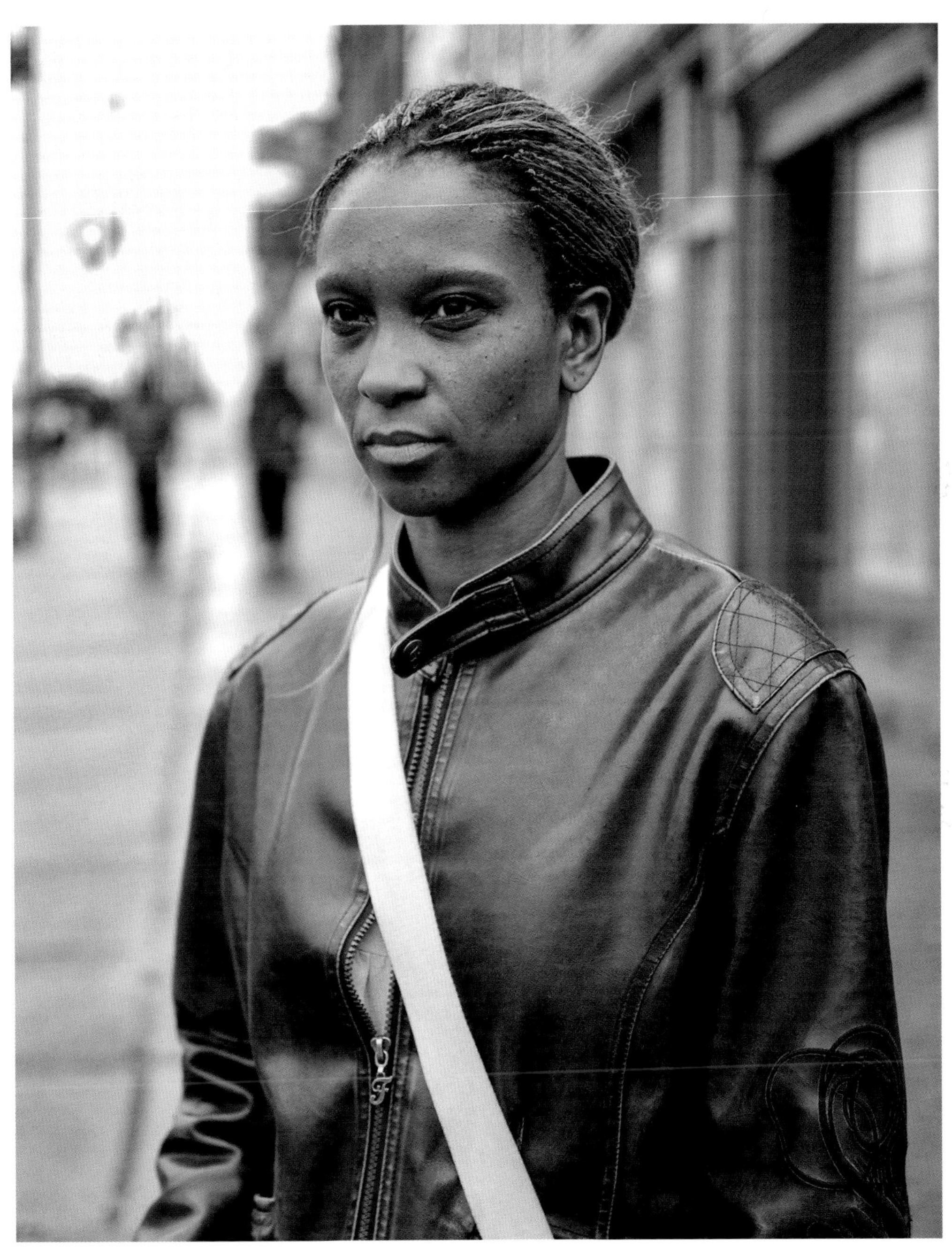

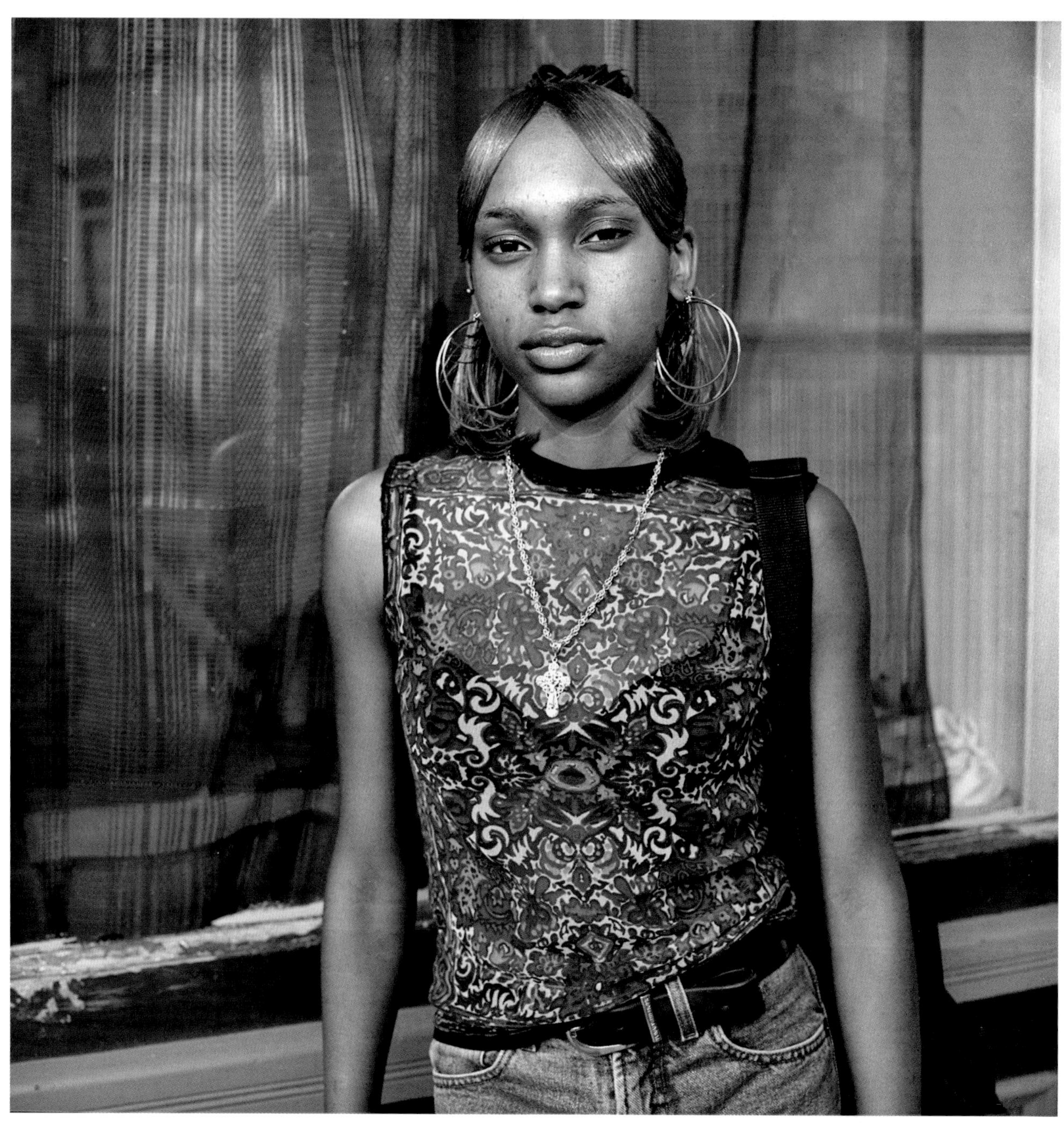

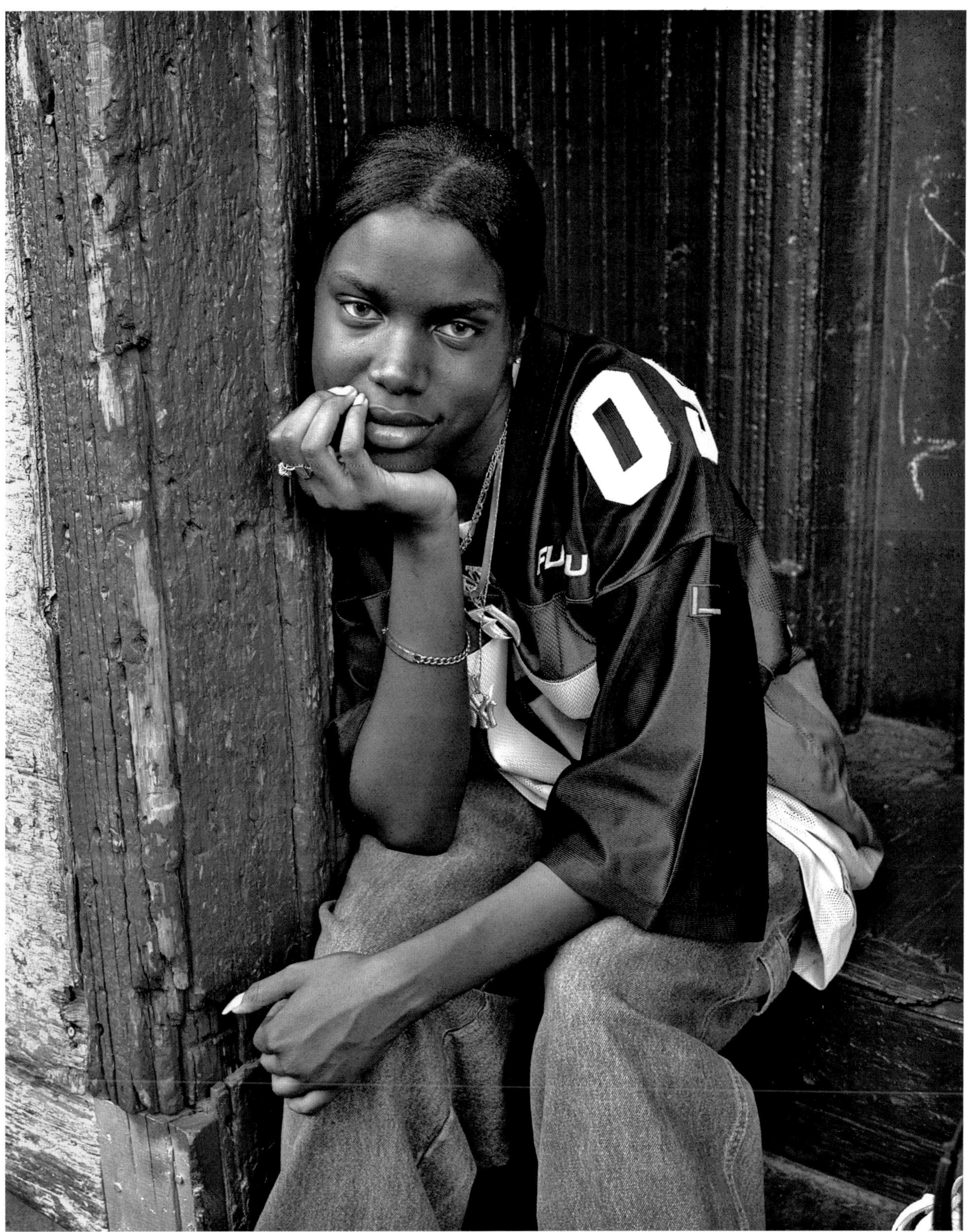

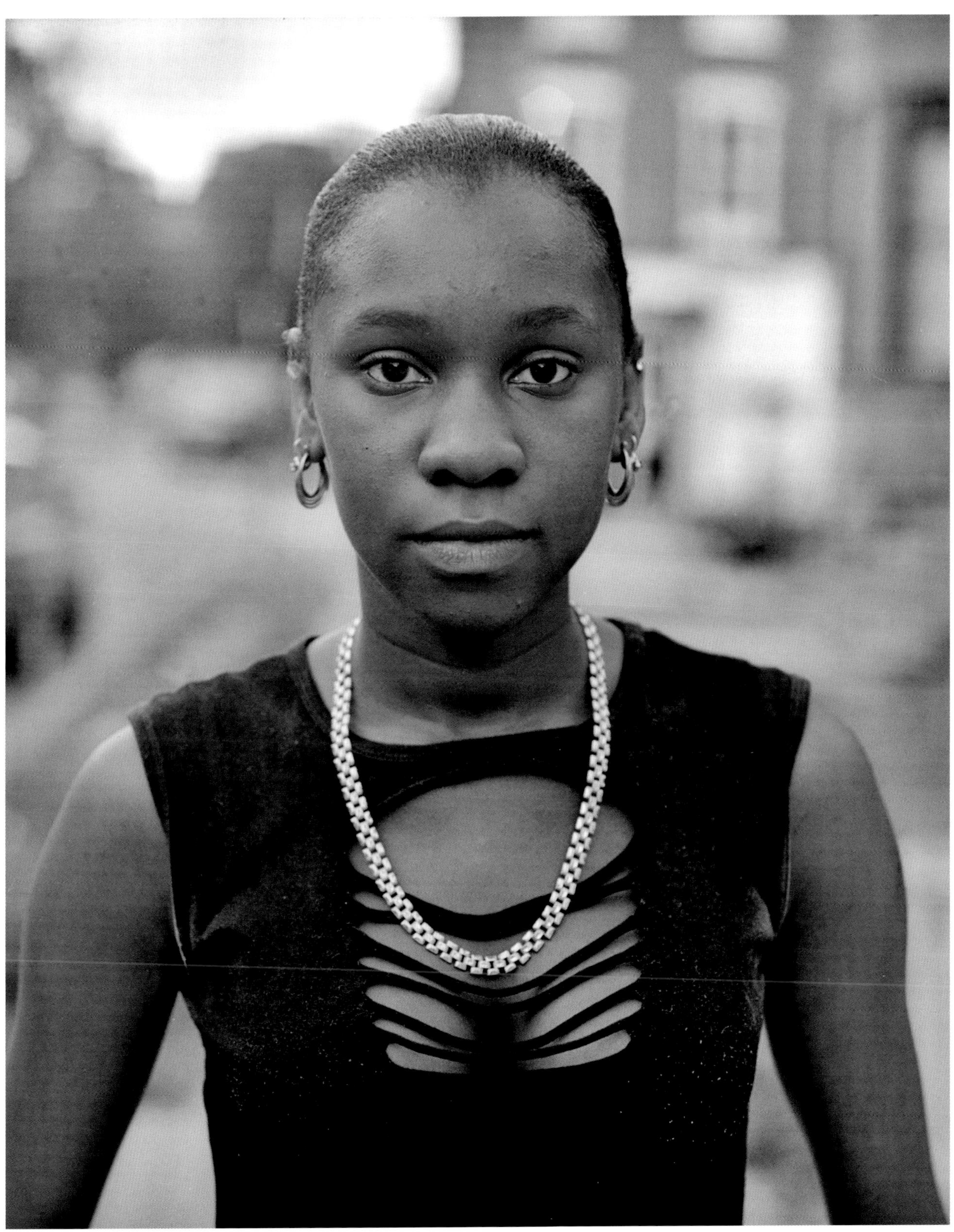

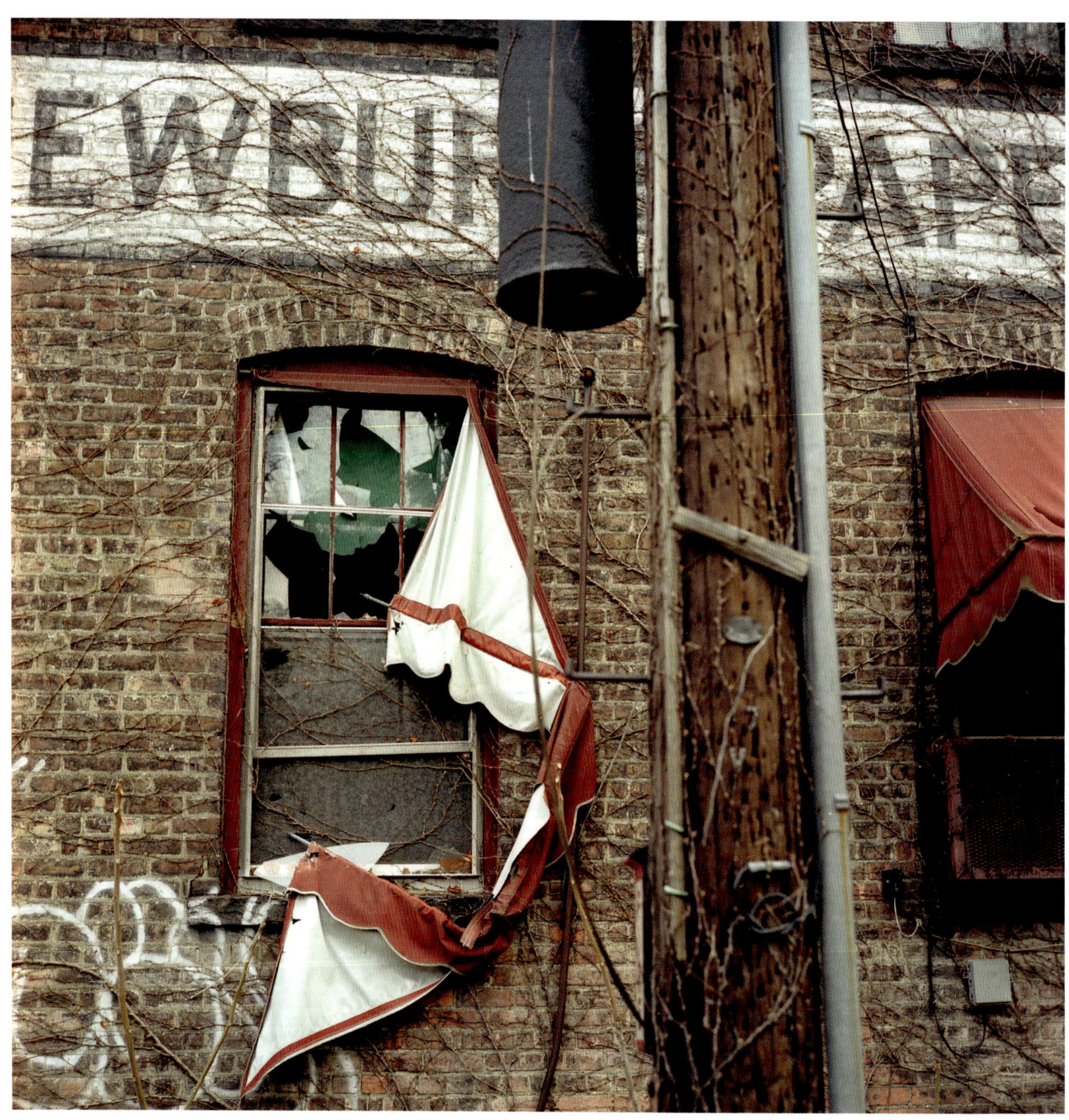

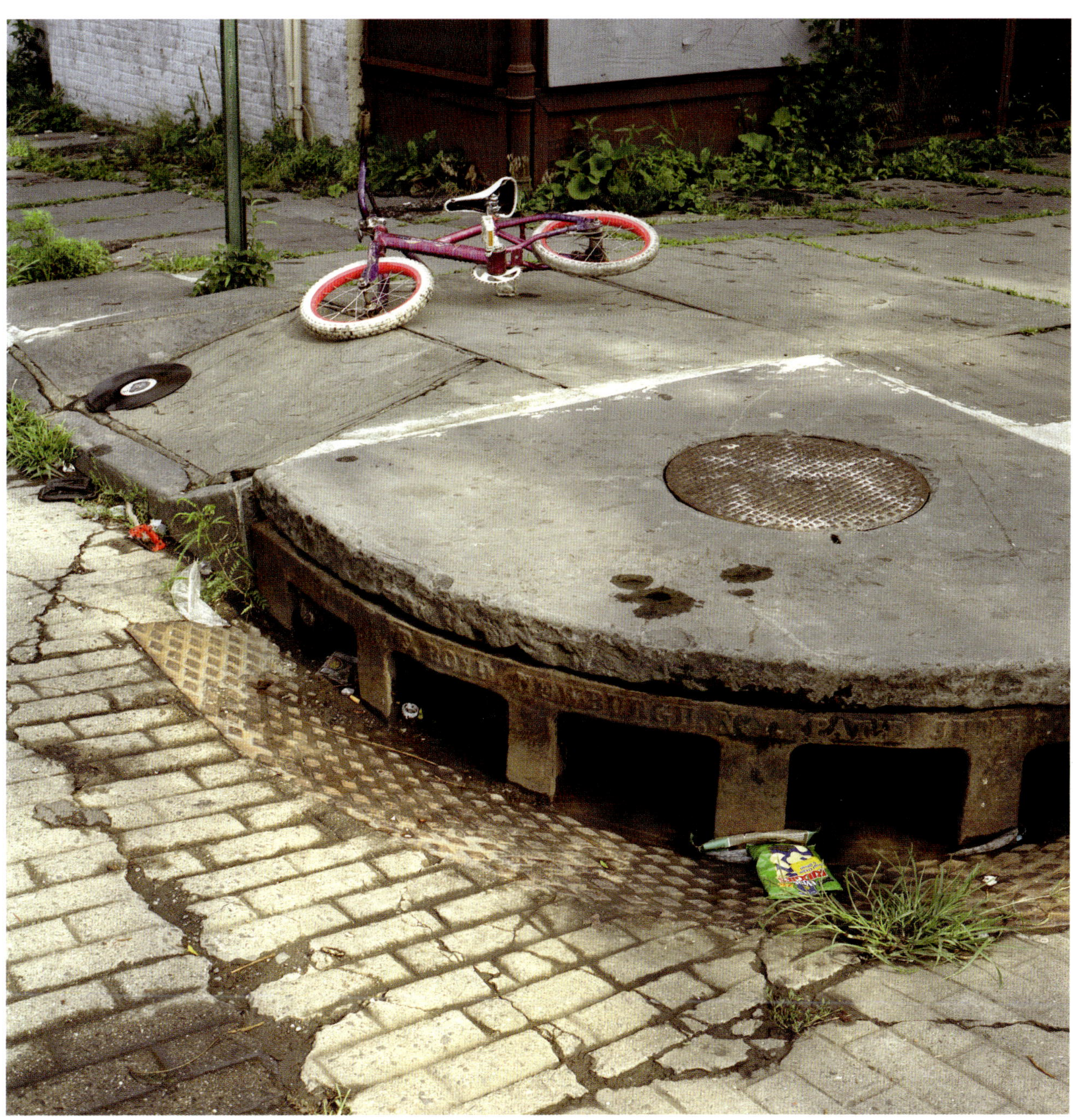

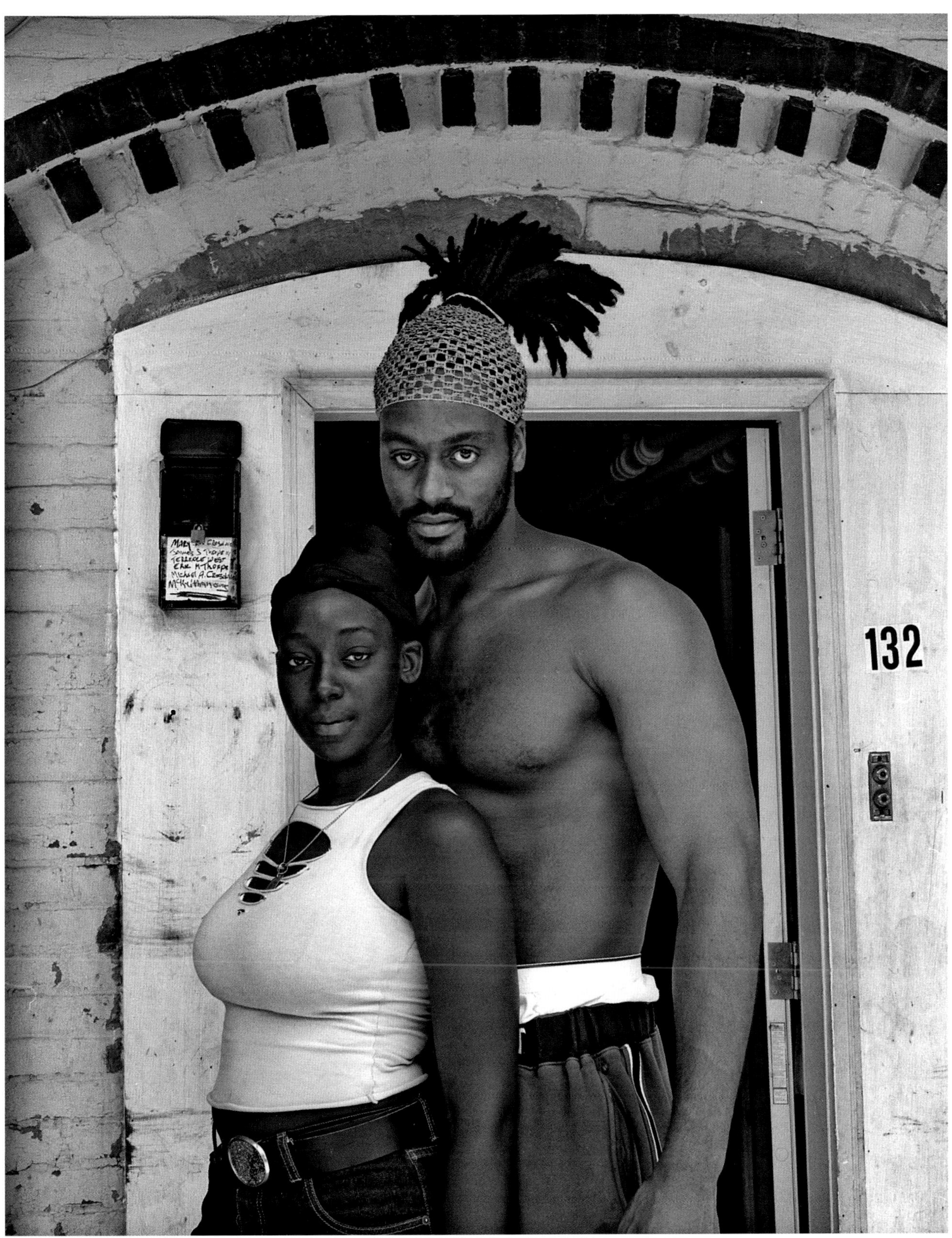
132

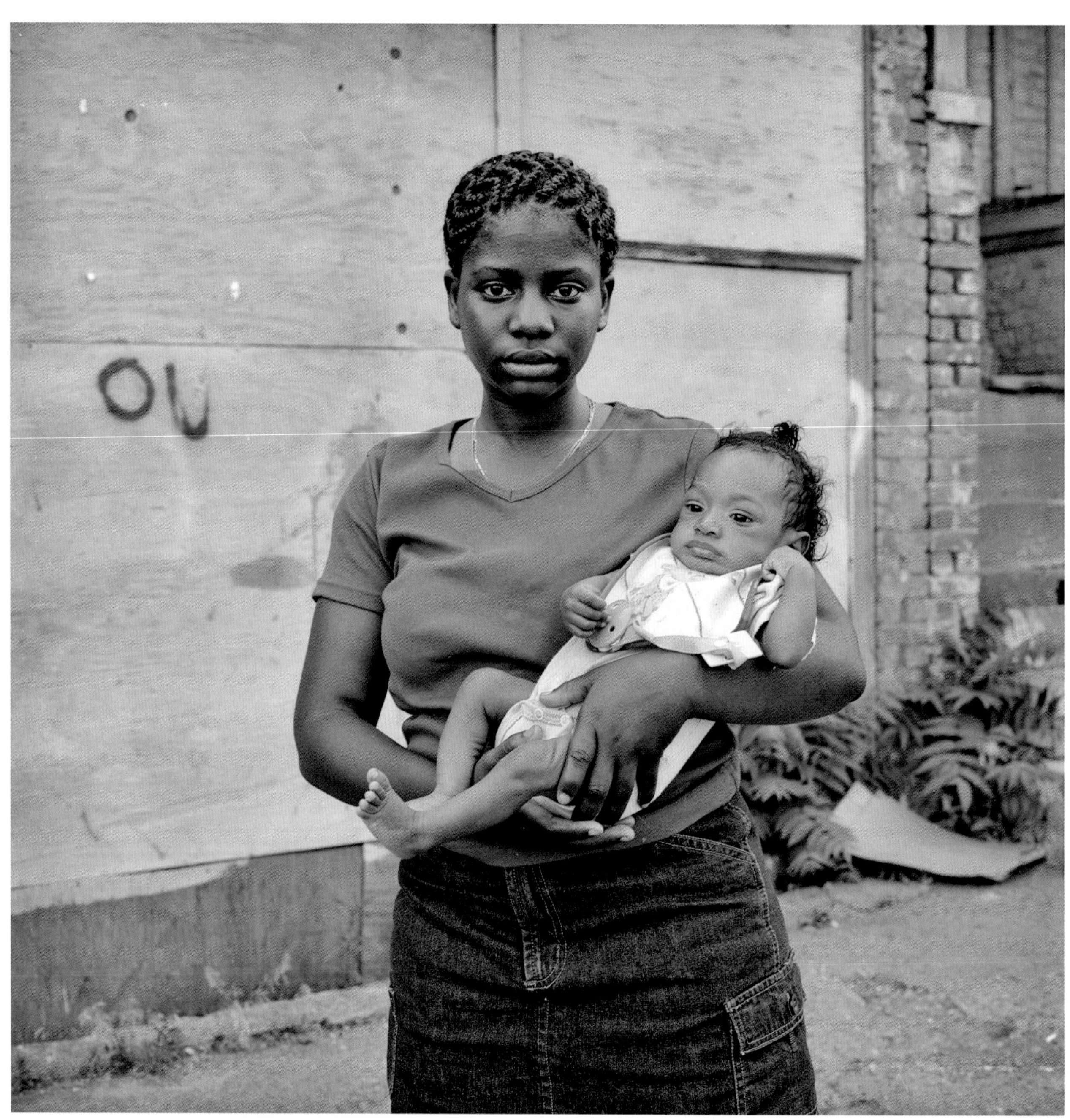
OU

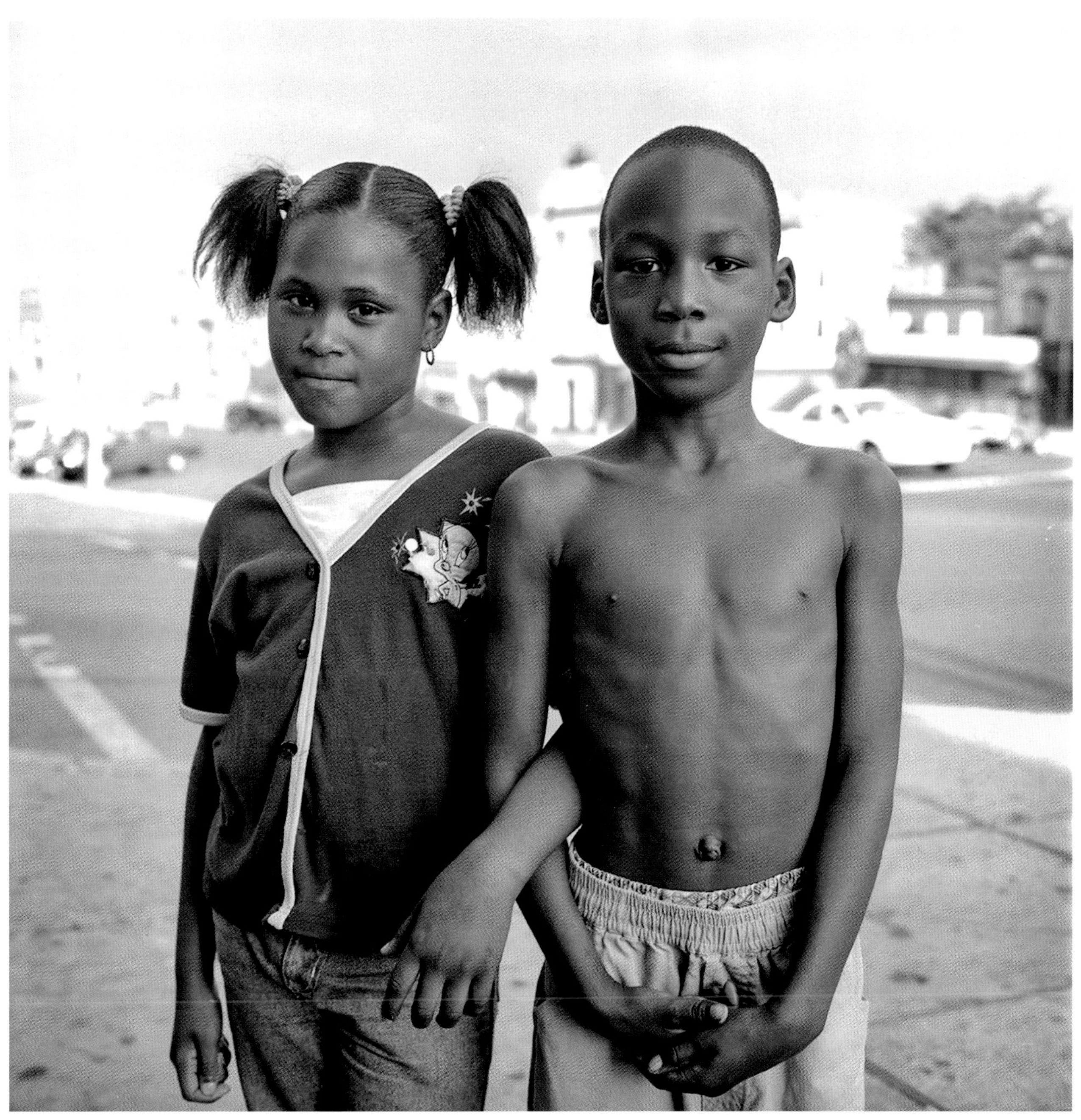

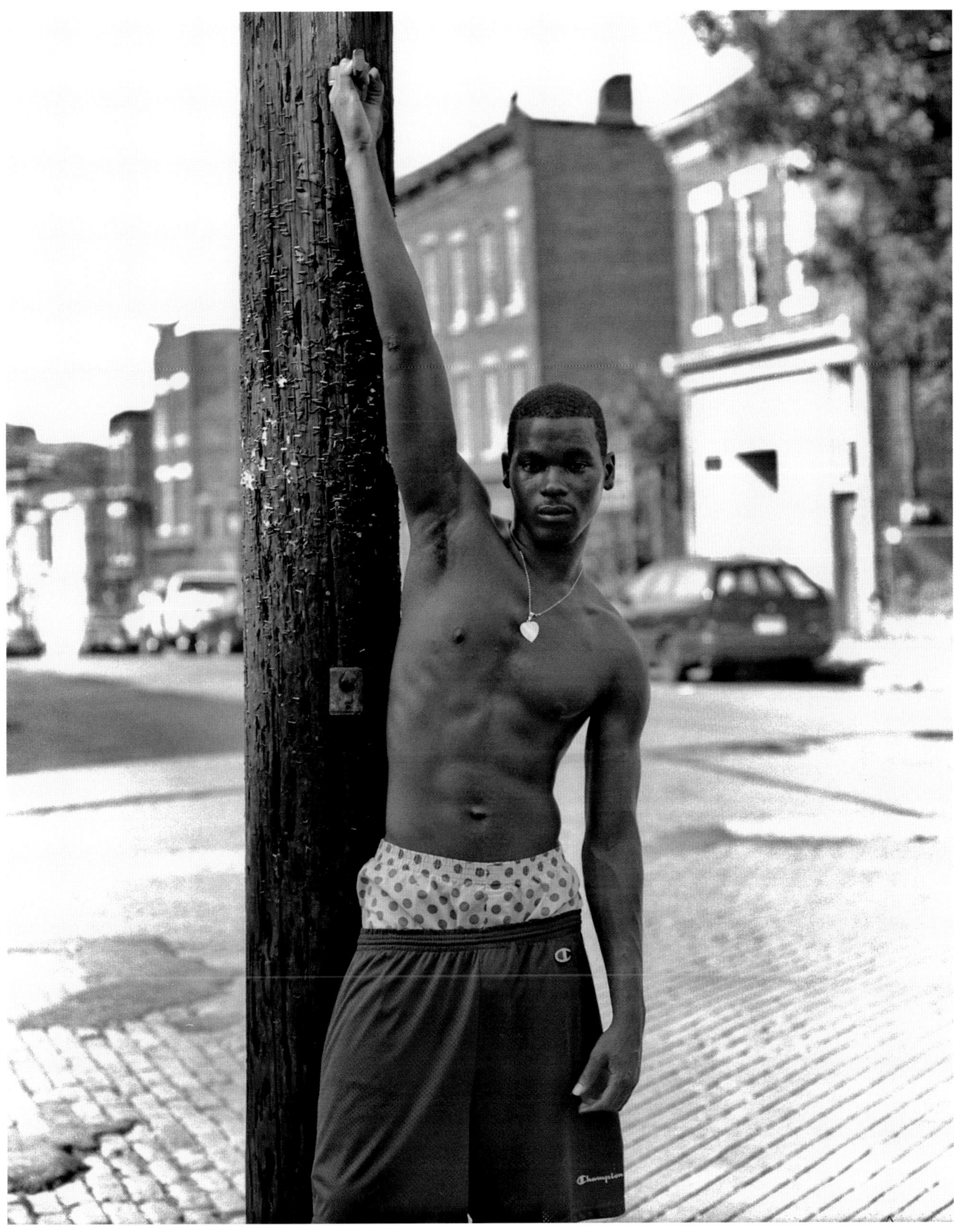
Champion

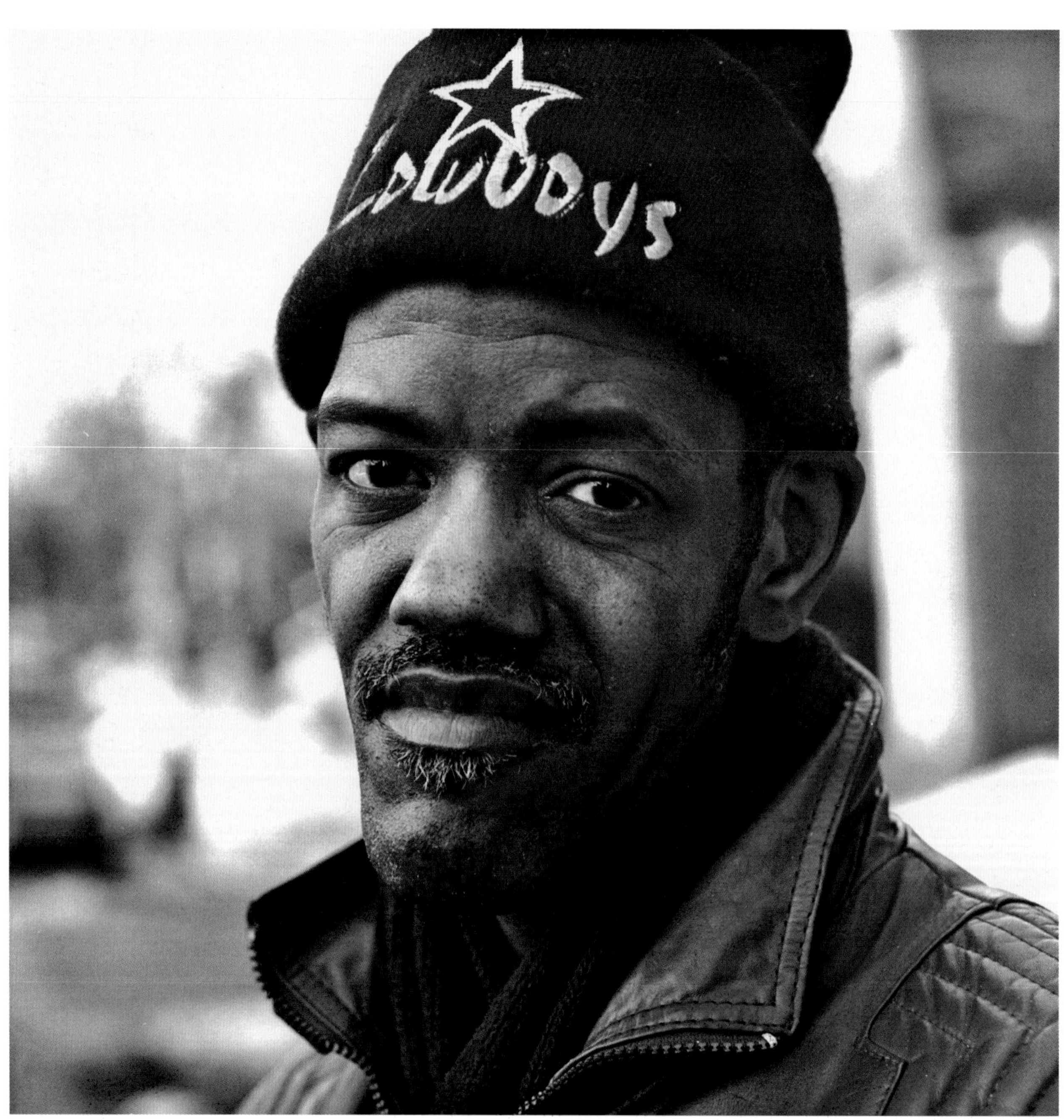

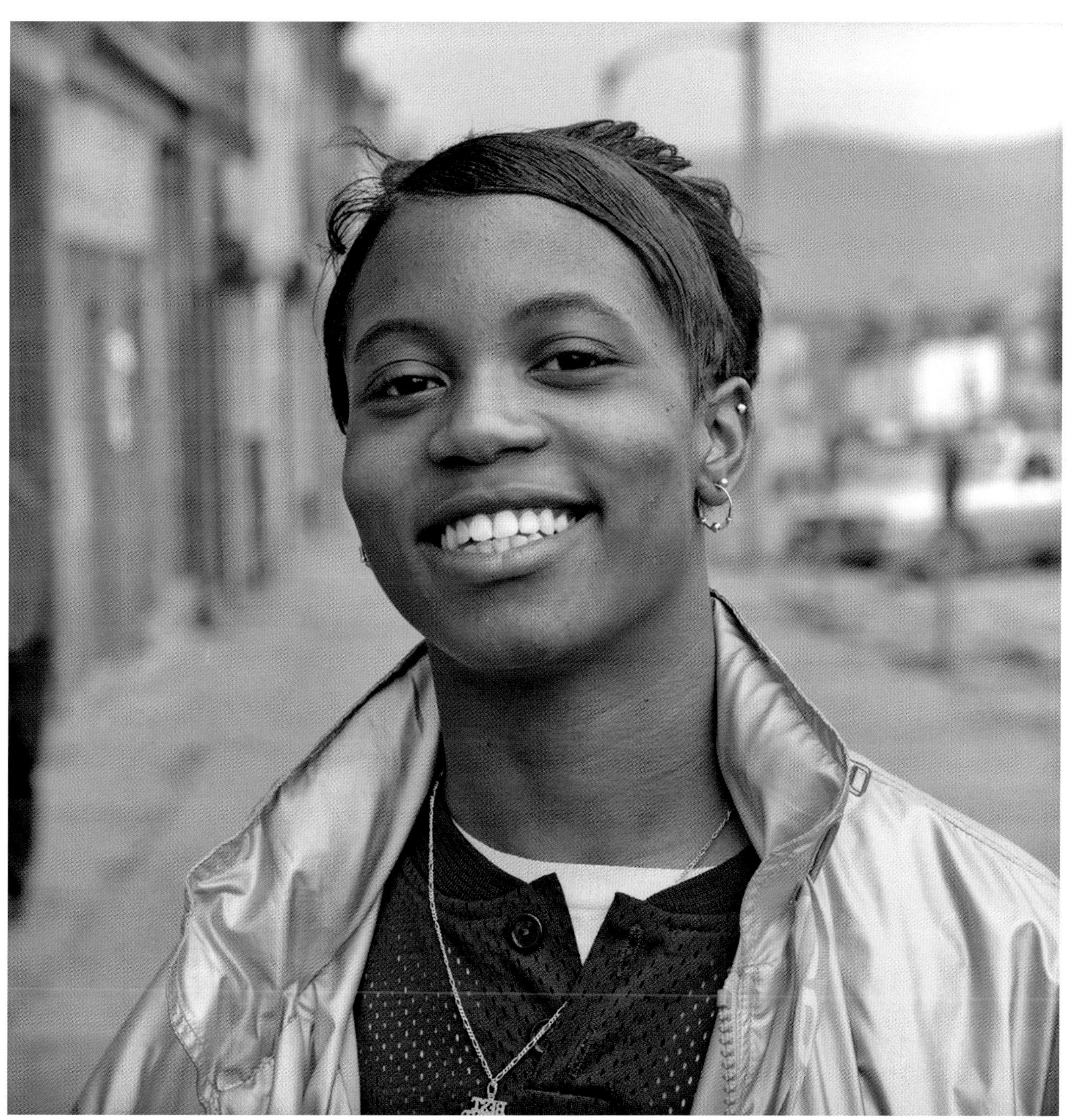

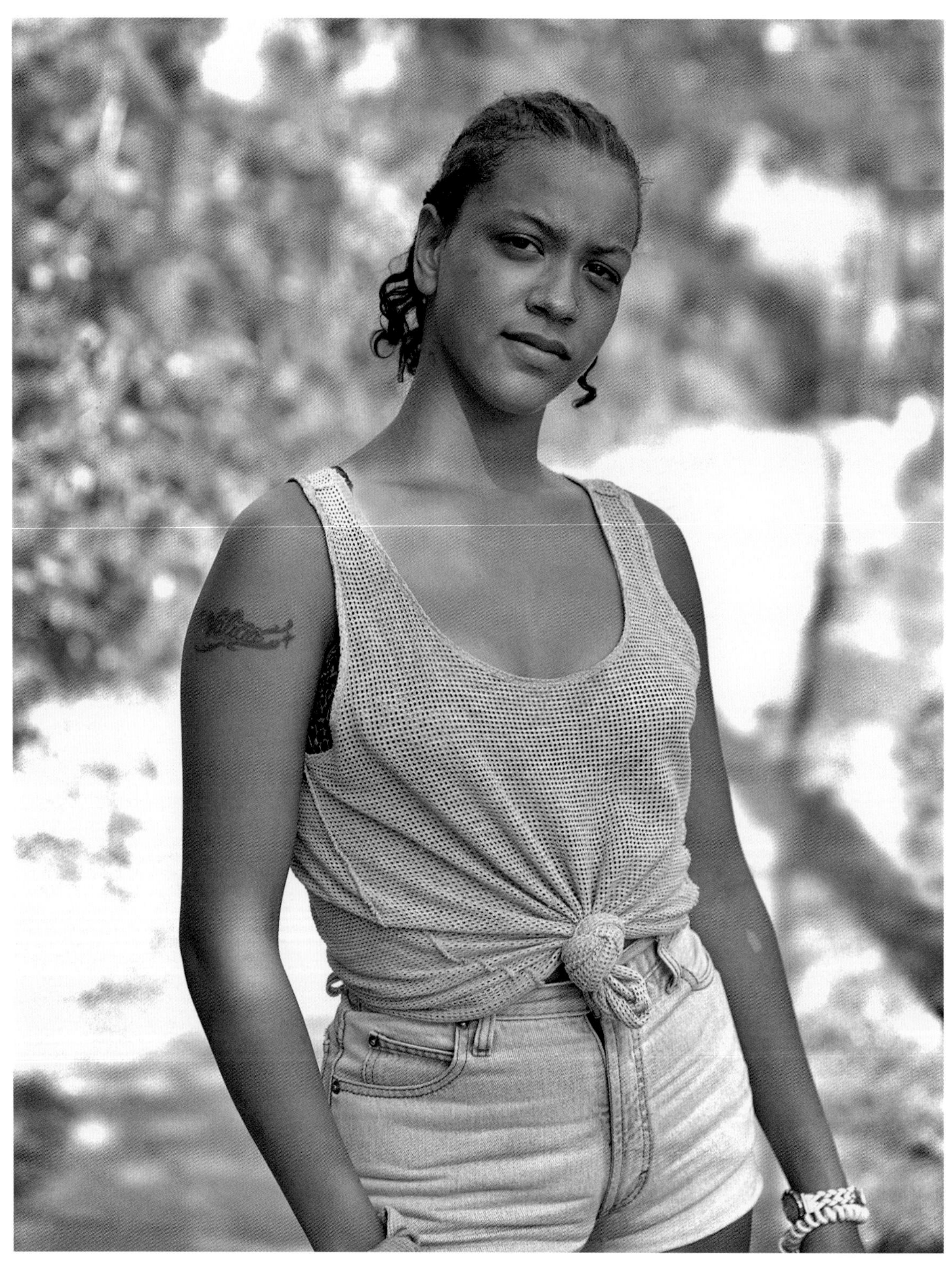

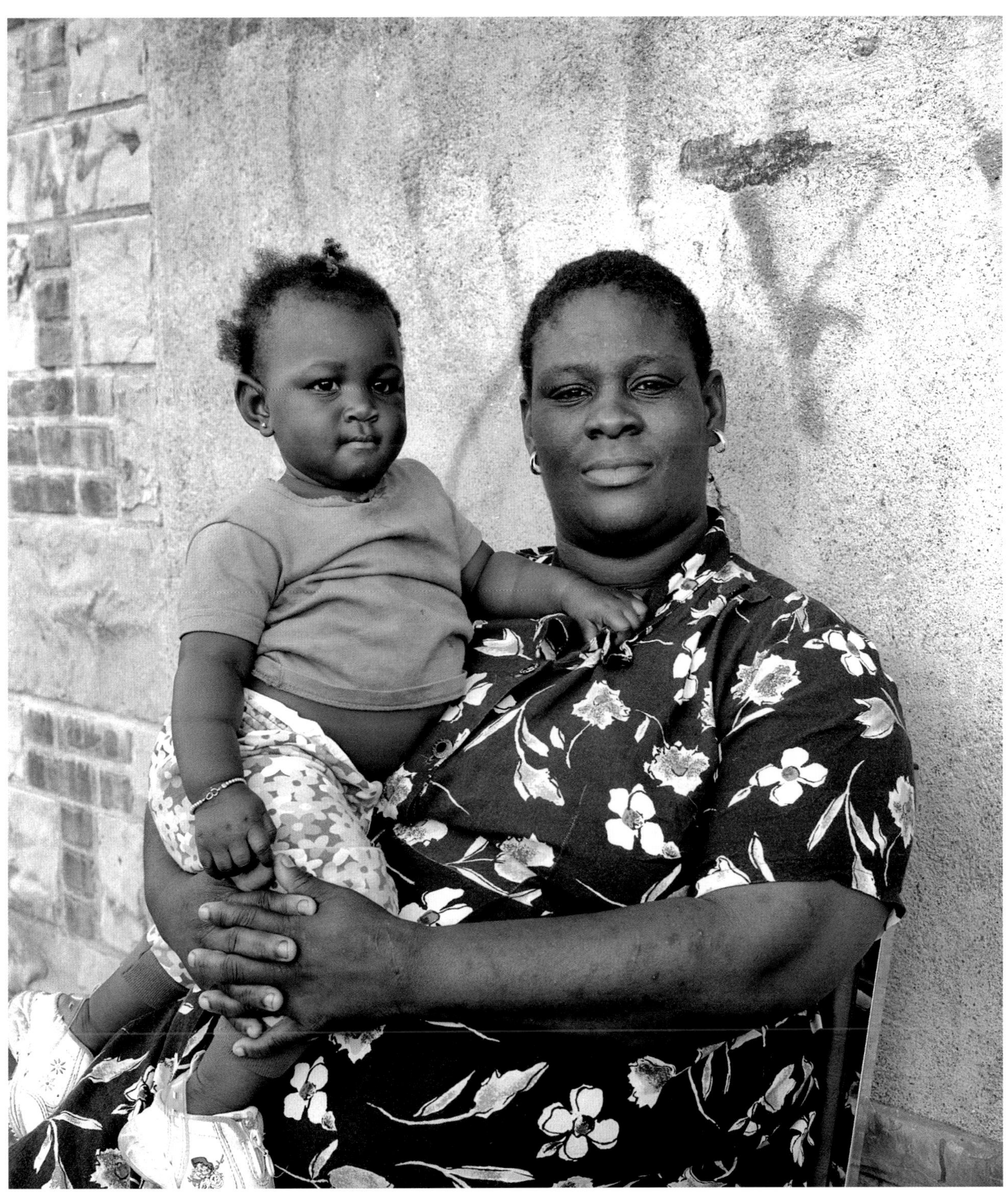

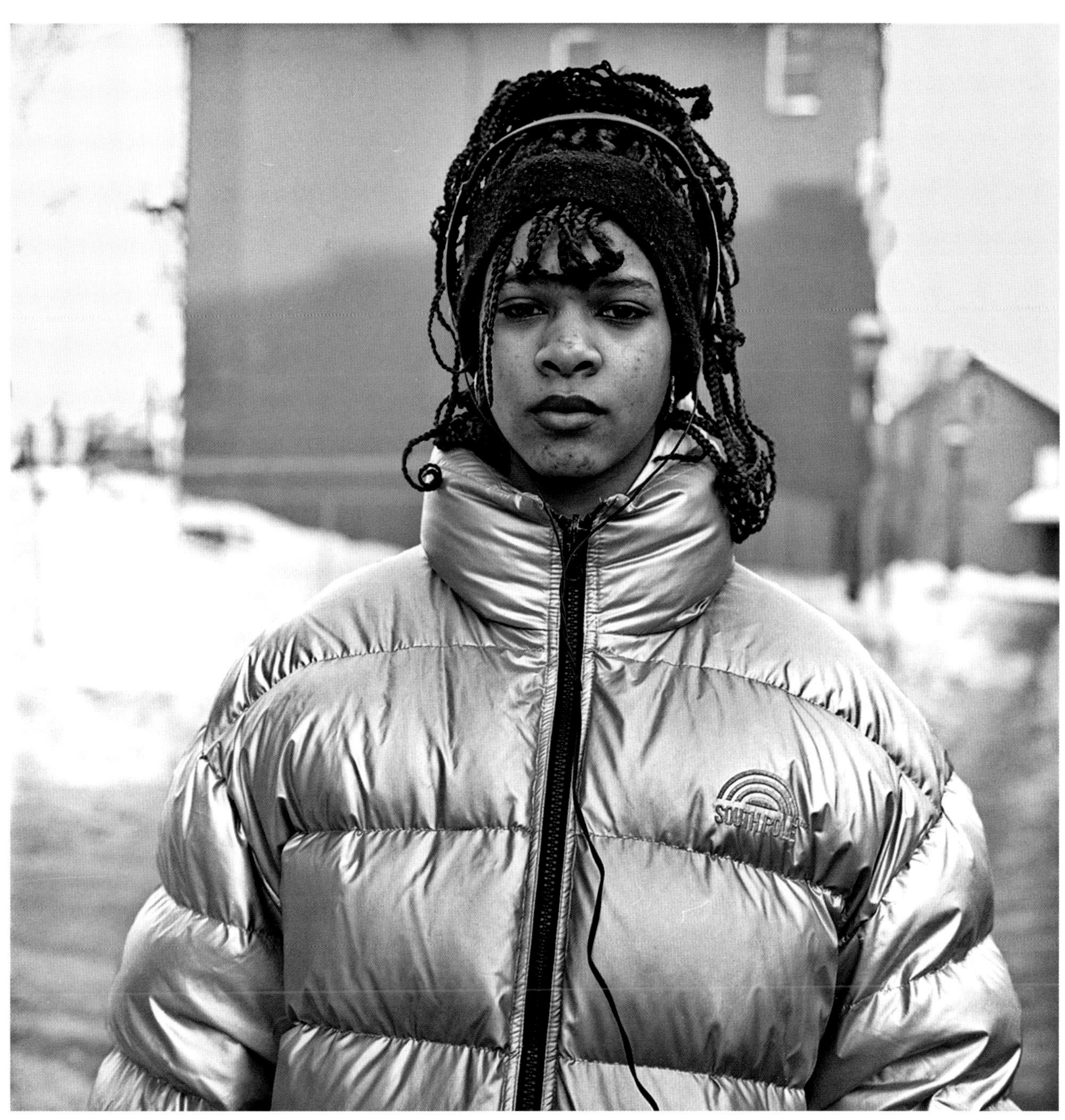
SOUTH POLE

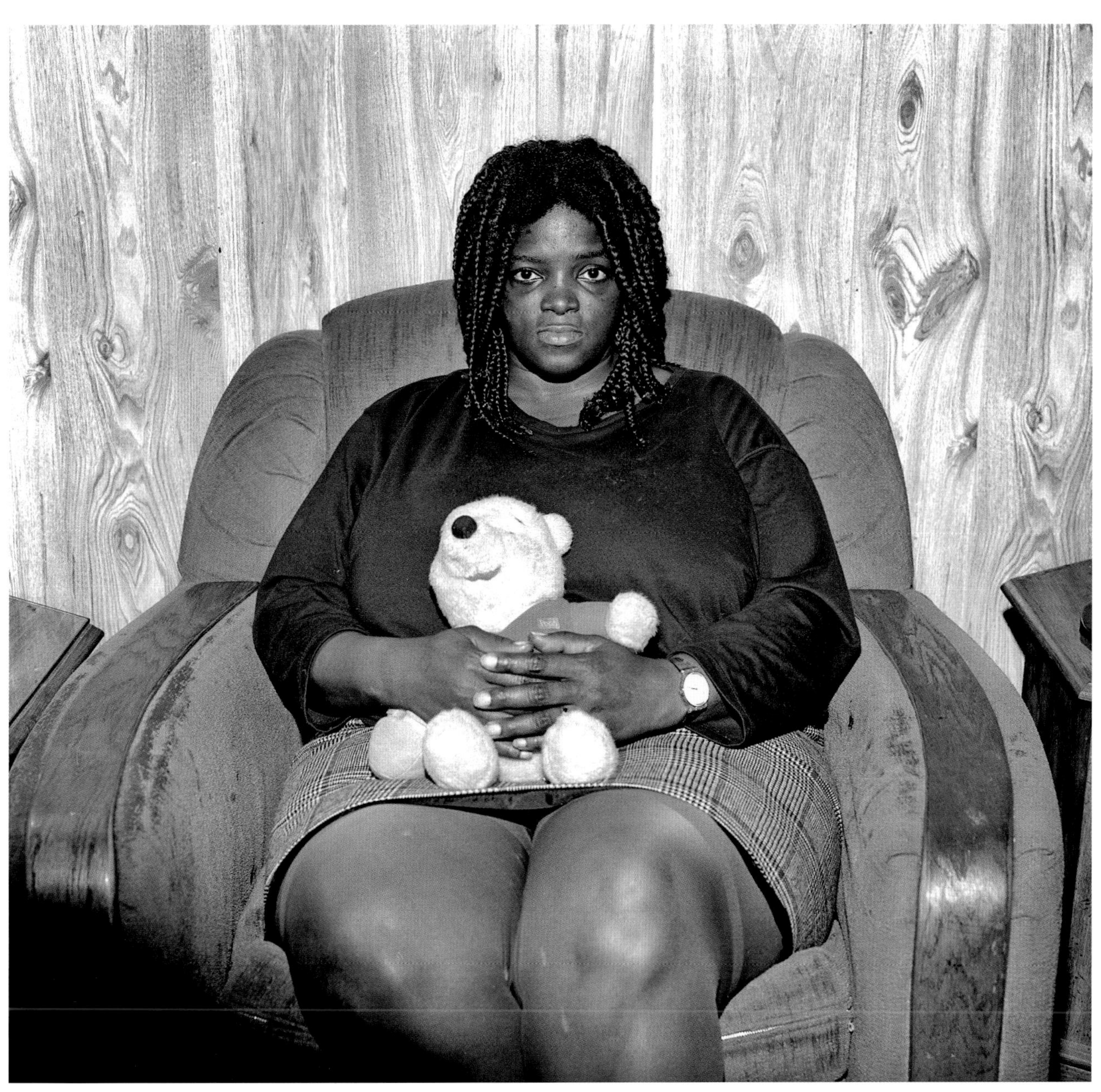

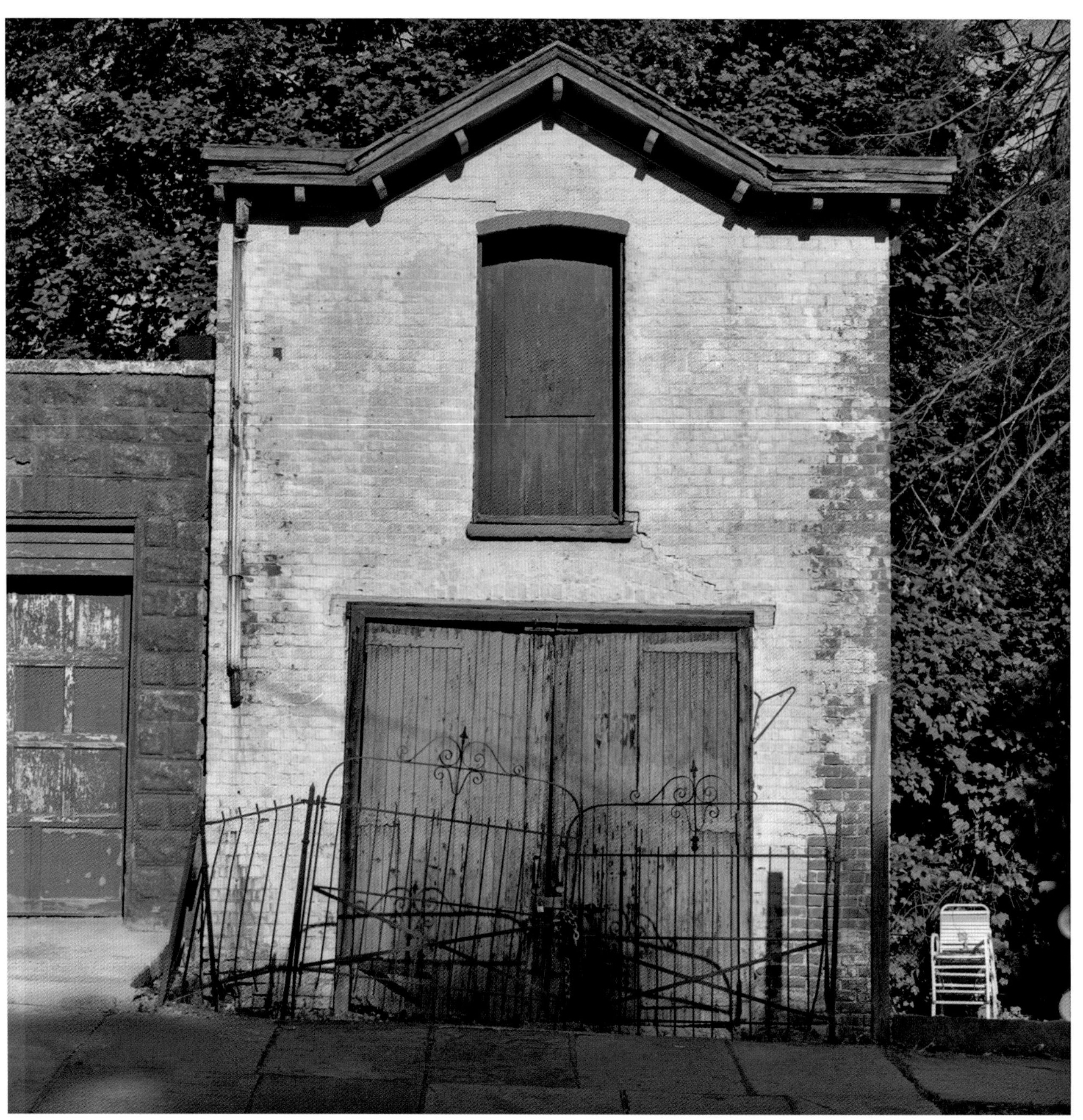

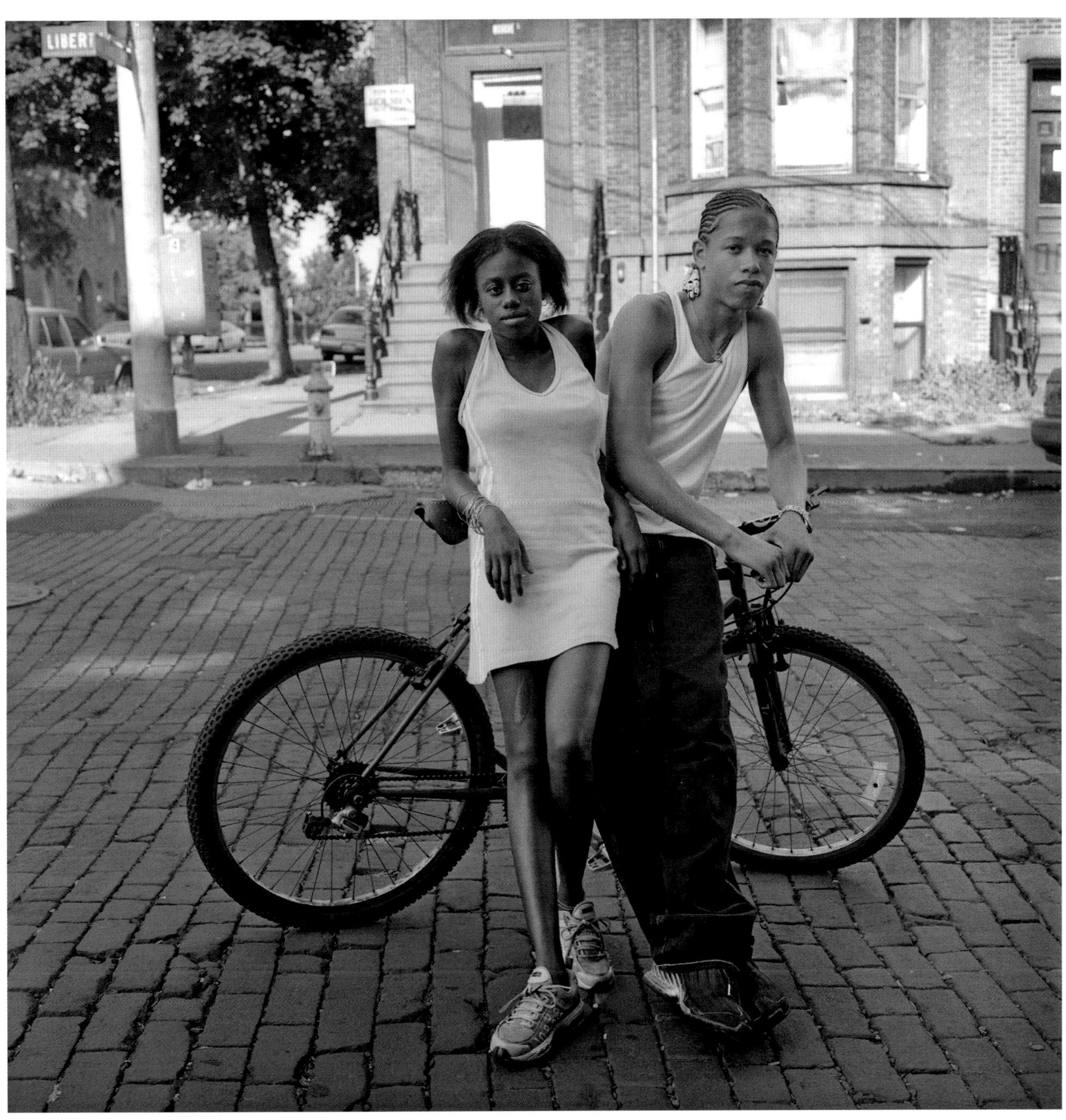

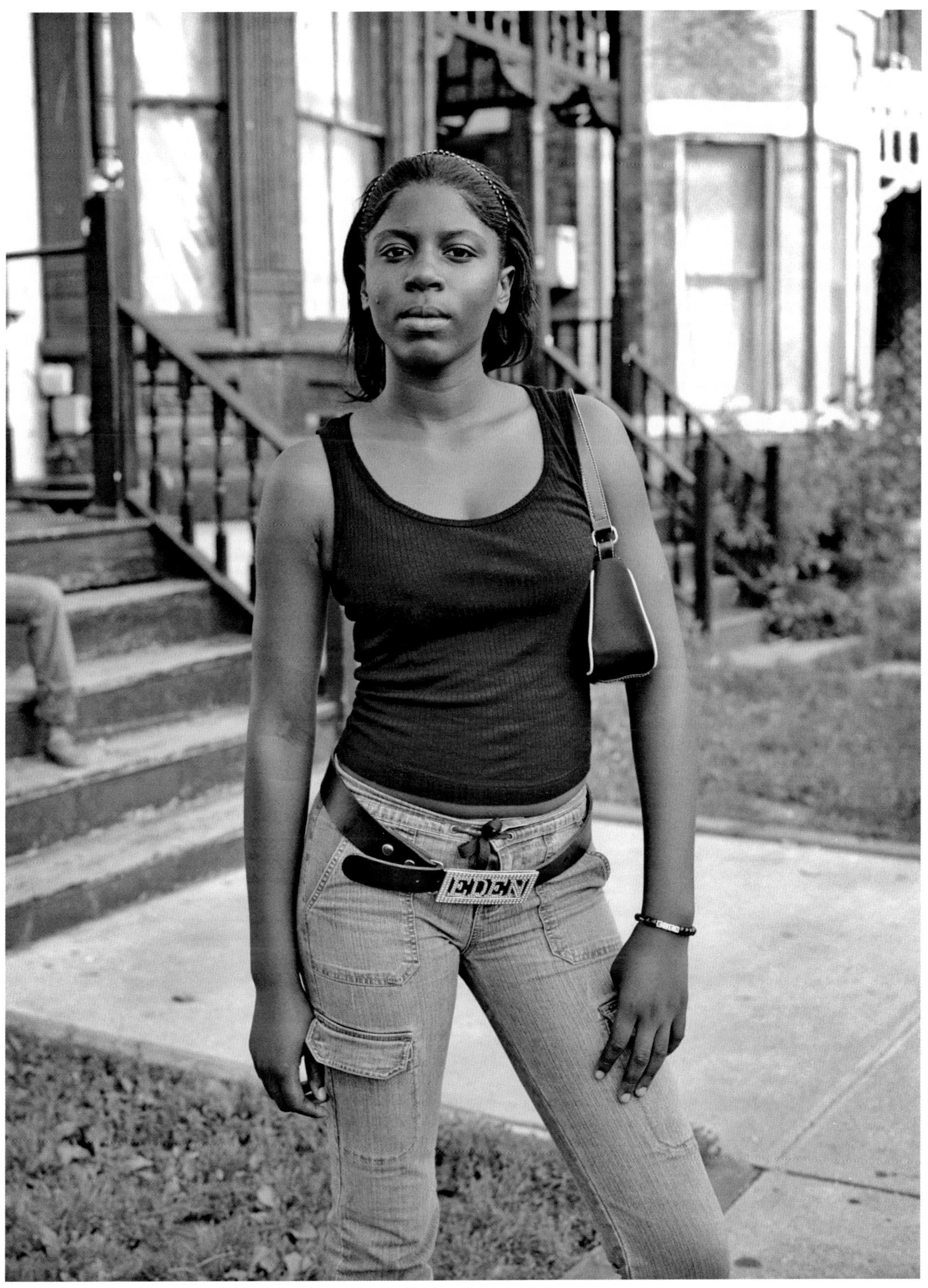
EDEN

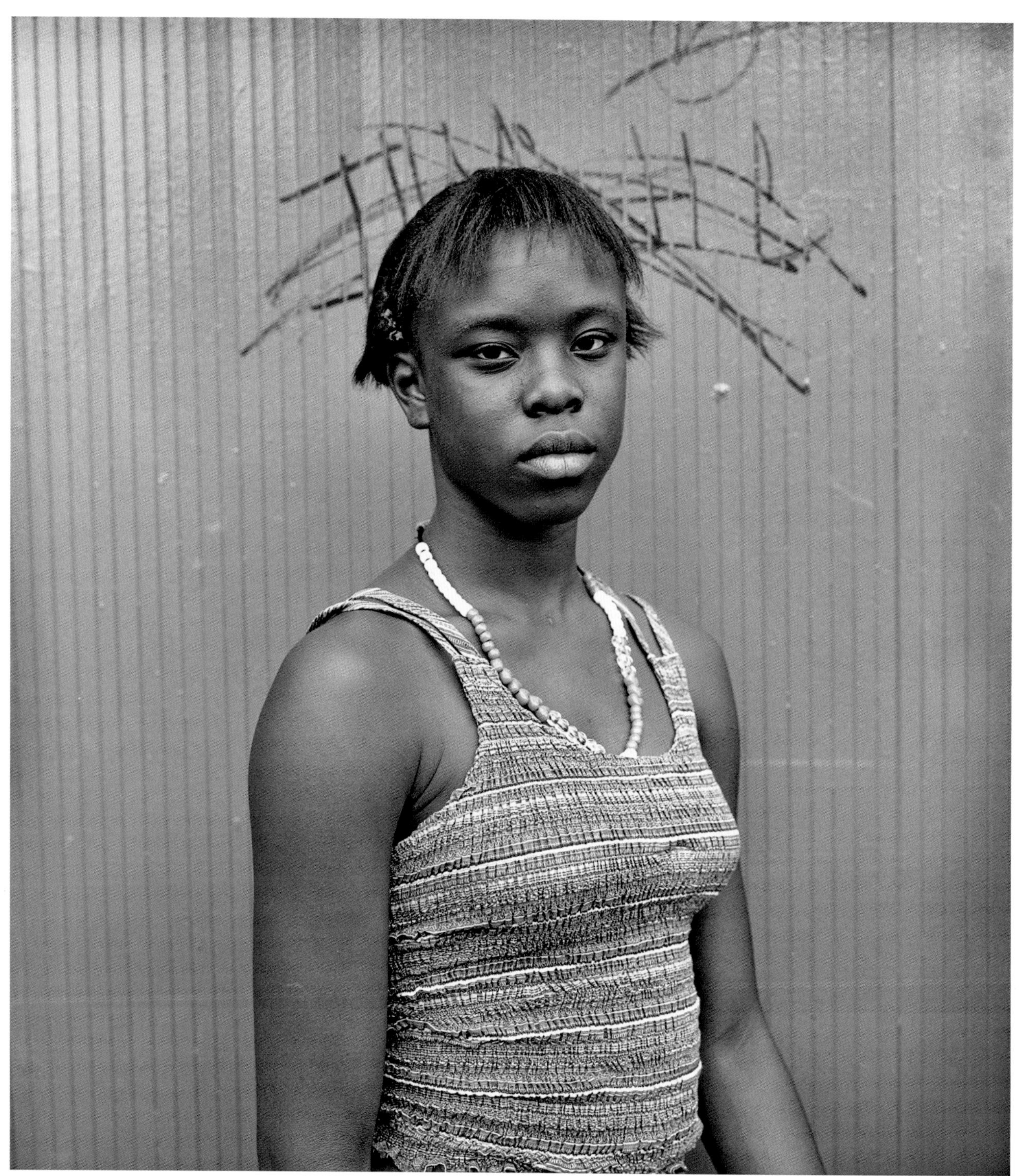

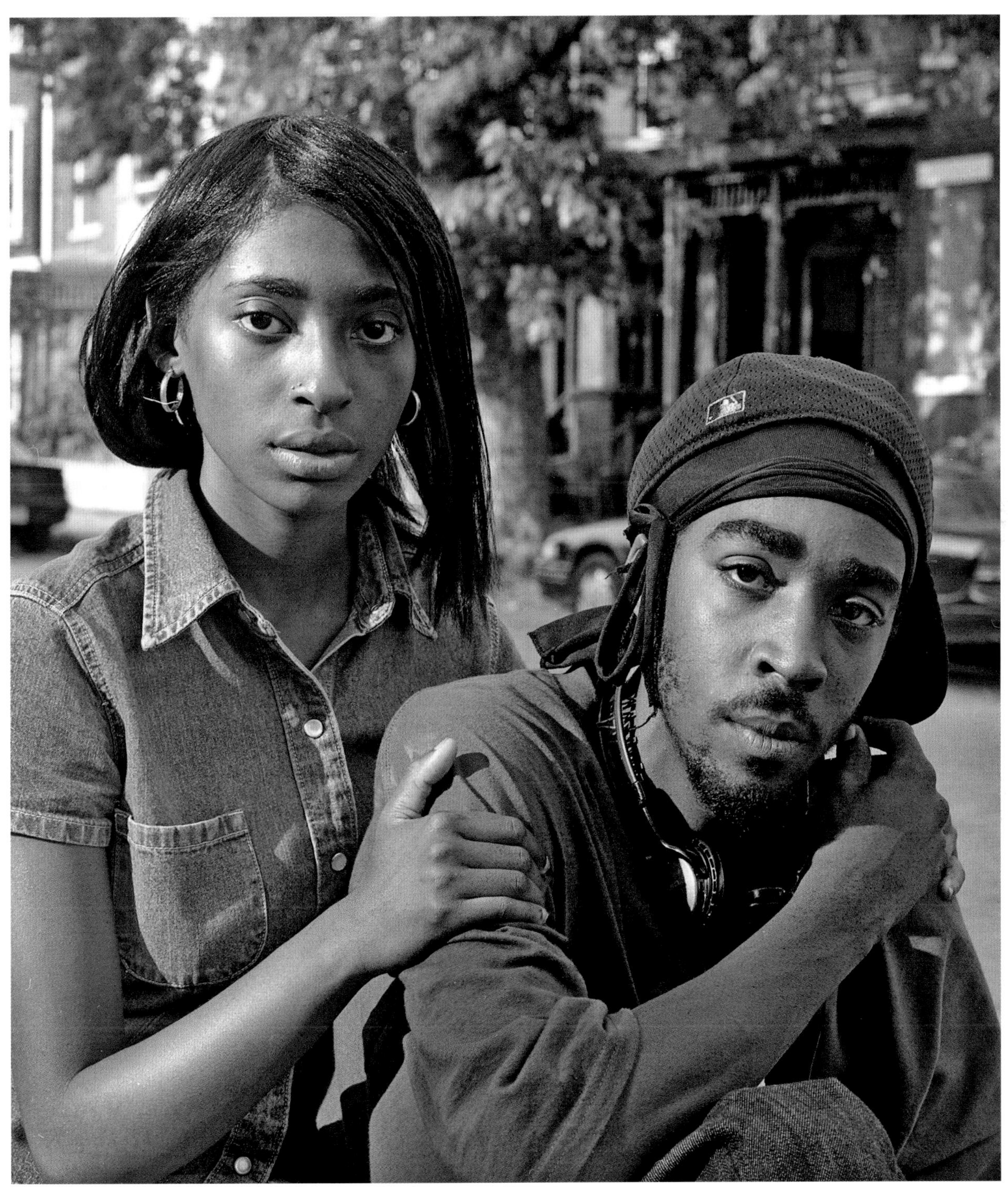

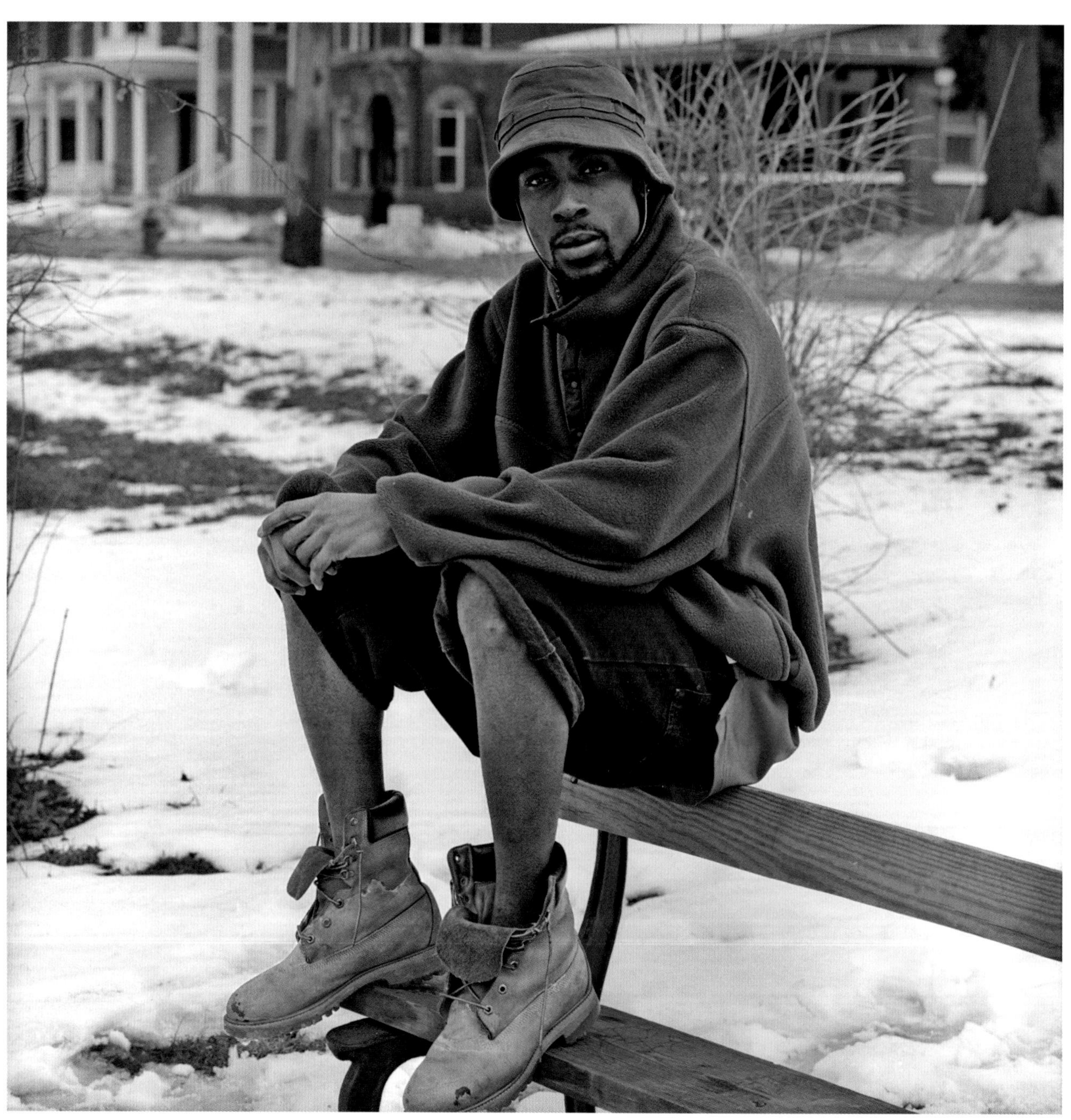

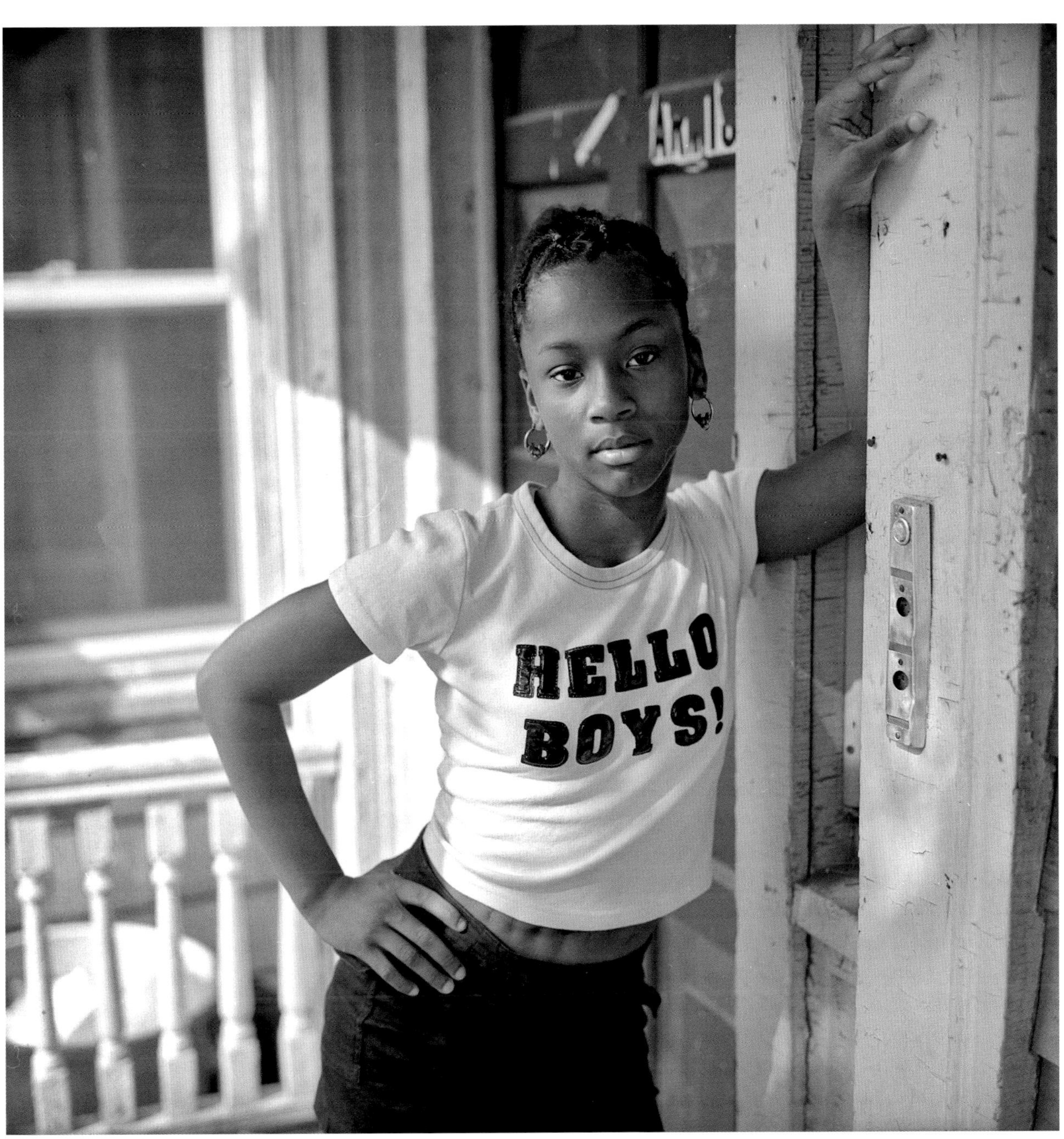
HELLO
BOYS!

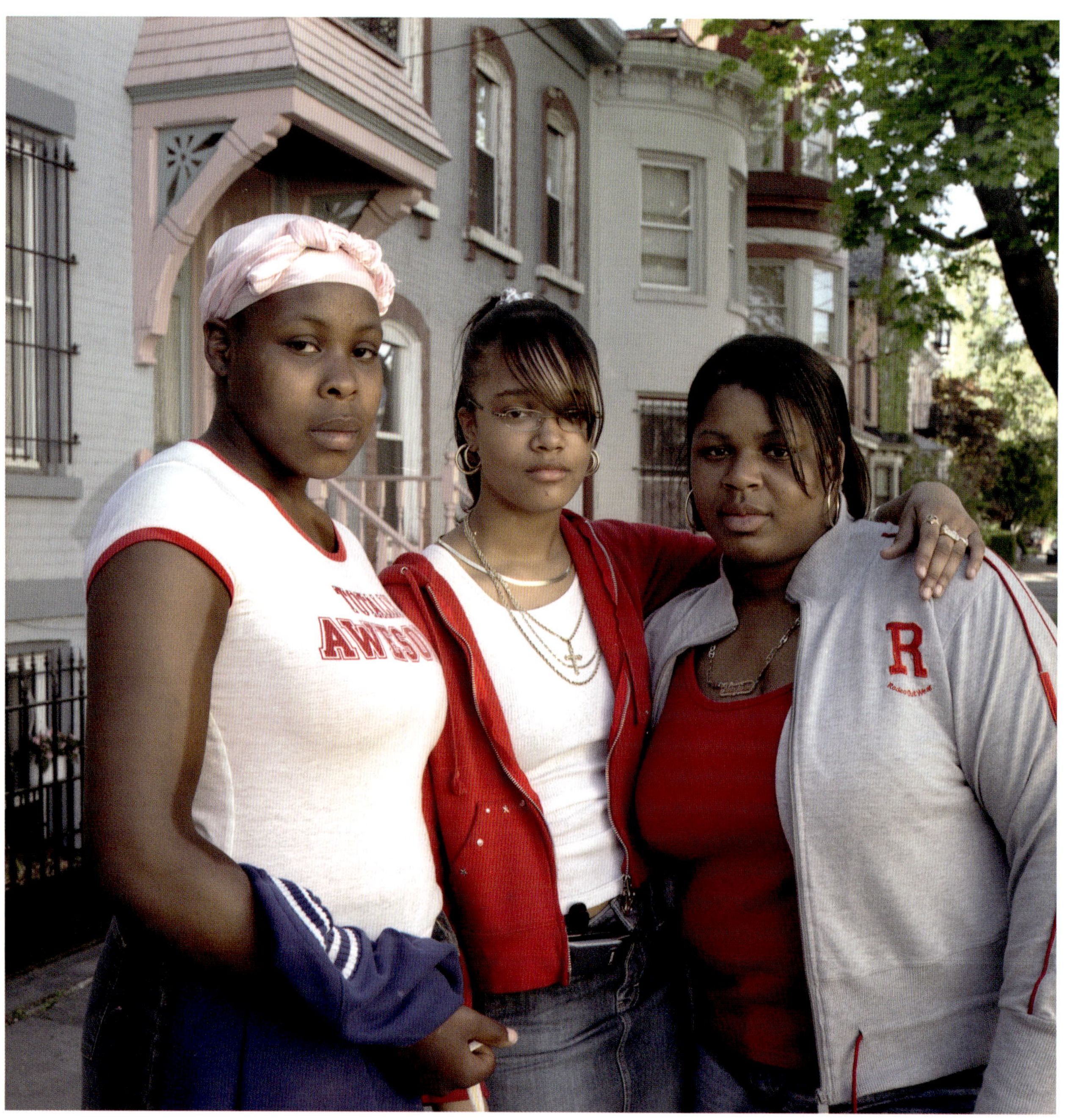

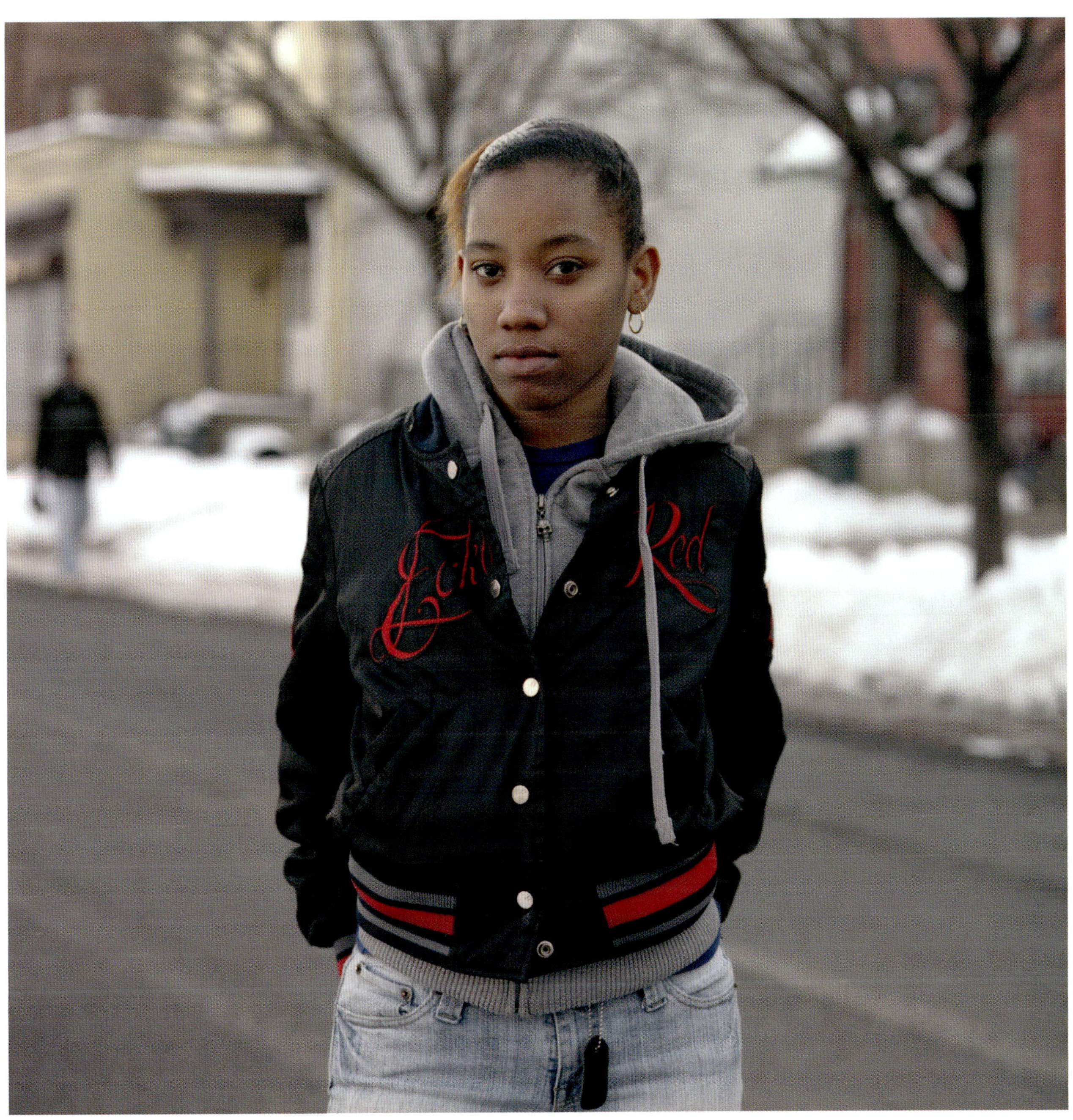
Red

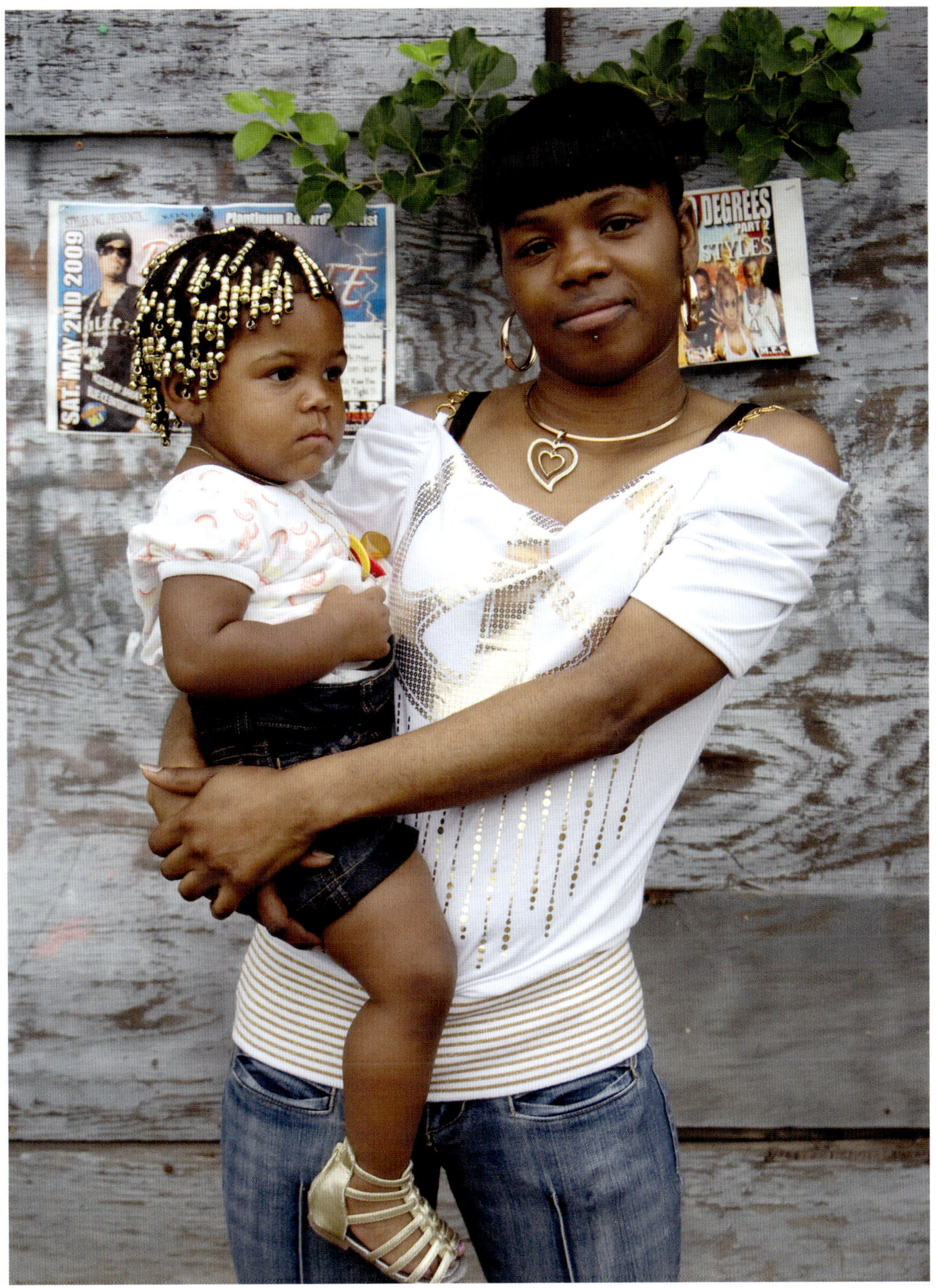
SAT. MAY 2ND 2009
DEGREES
PART 2
STYLES

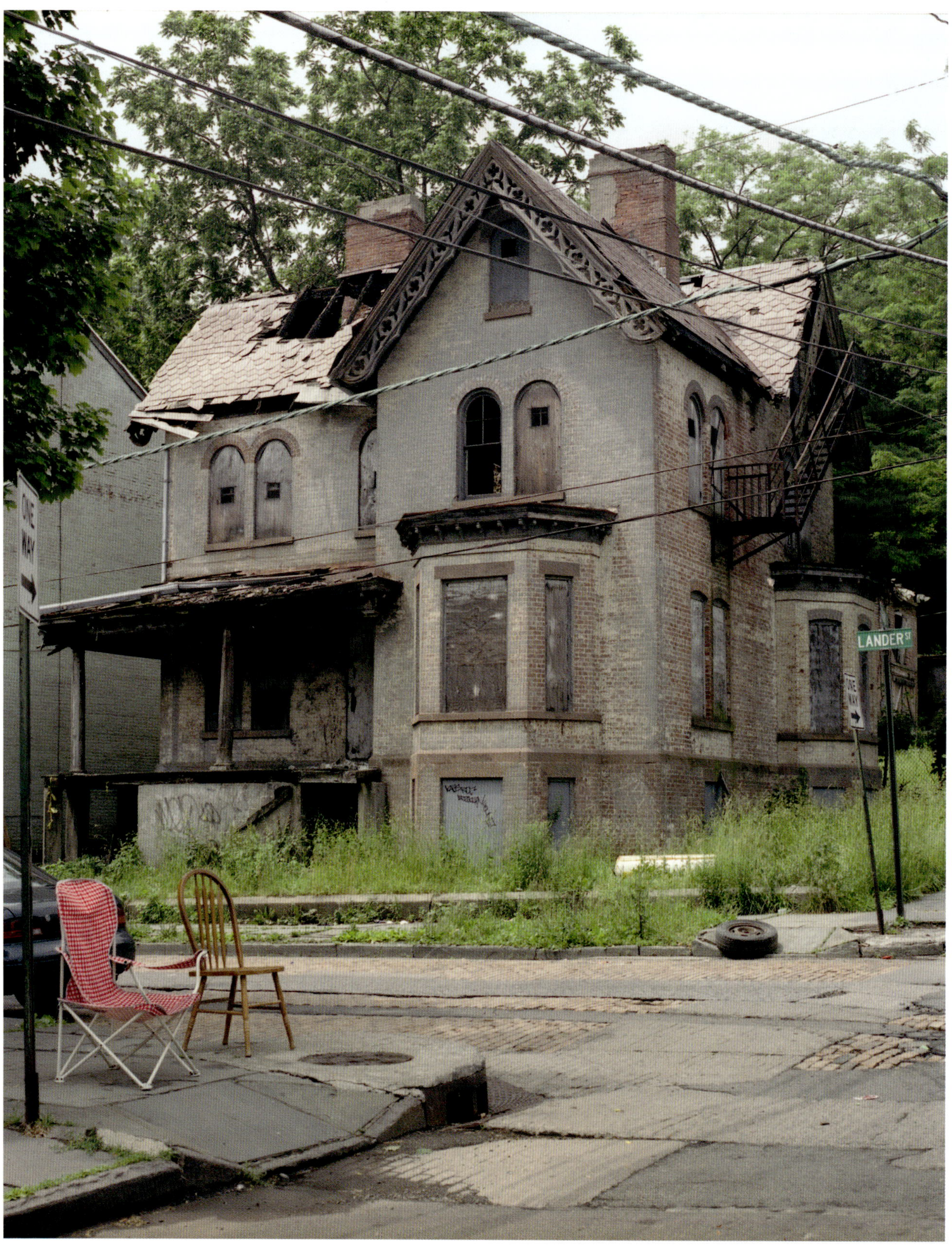
ONE WAY
LANDER ST
ONE WAY

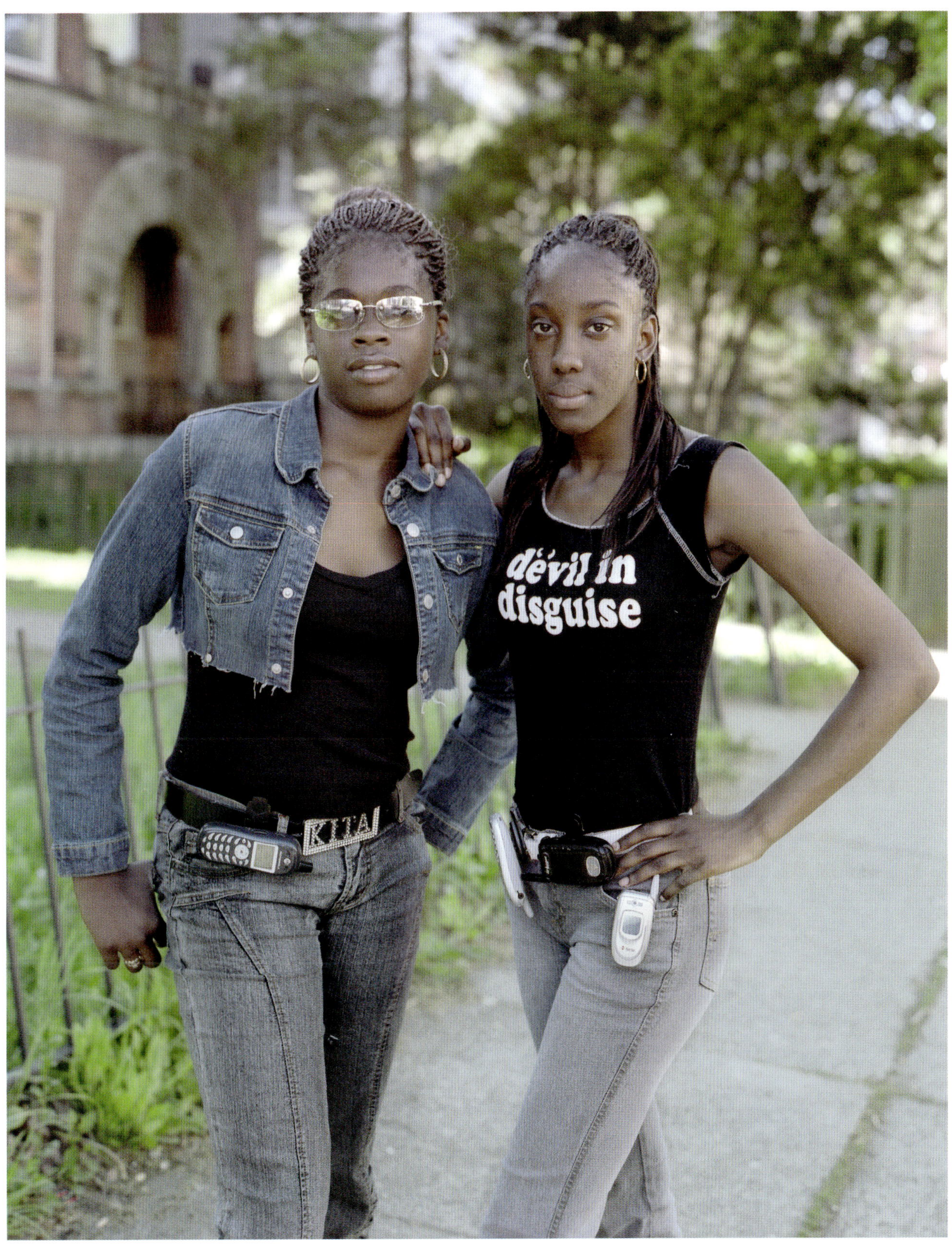
devil in
disguise
KITA

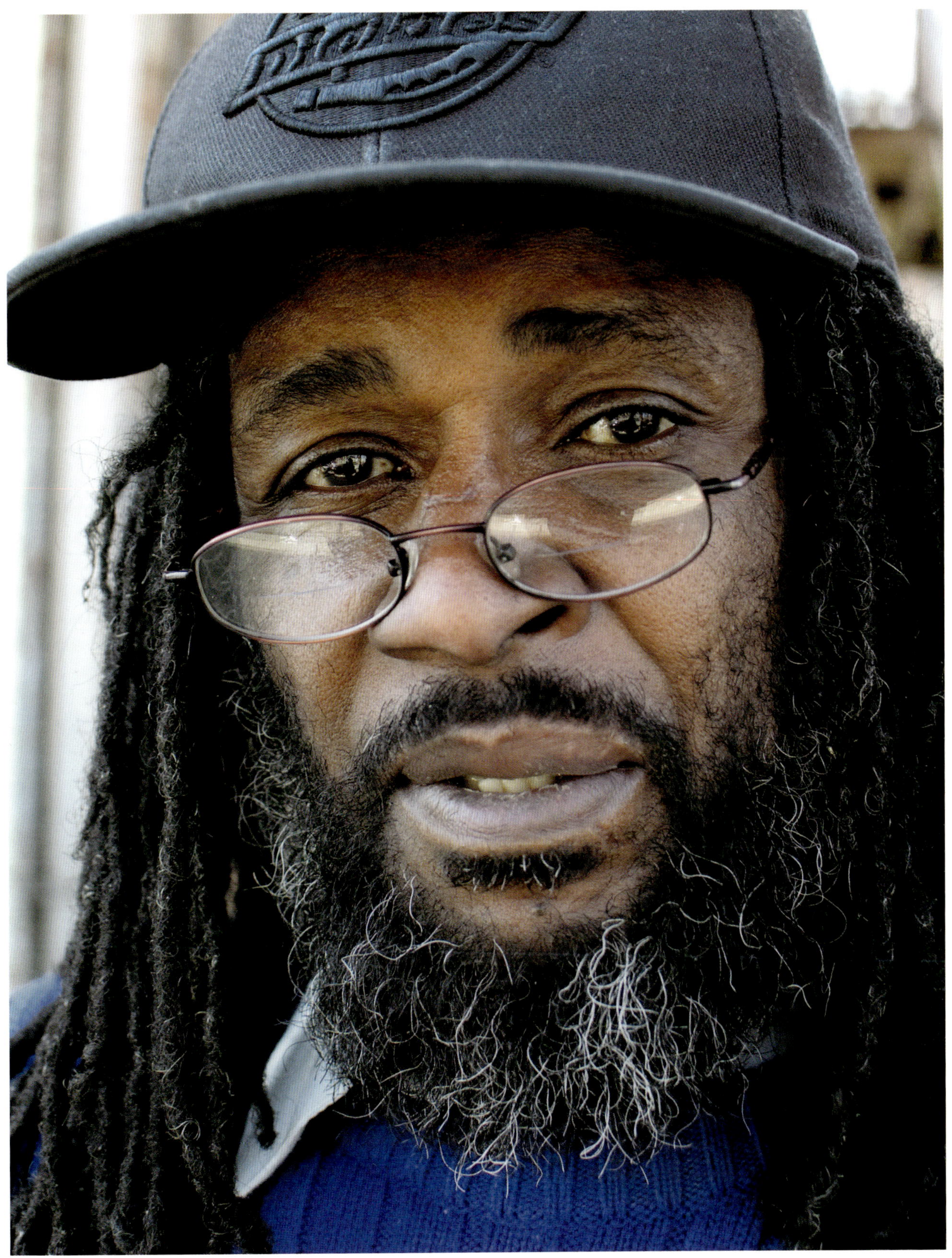

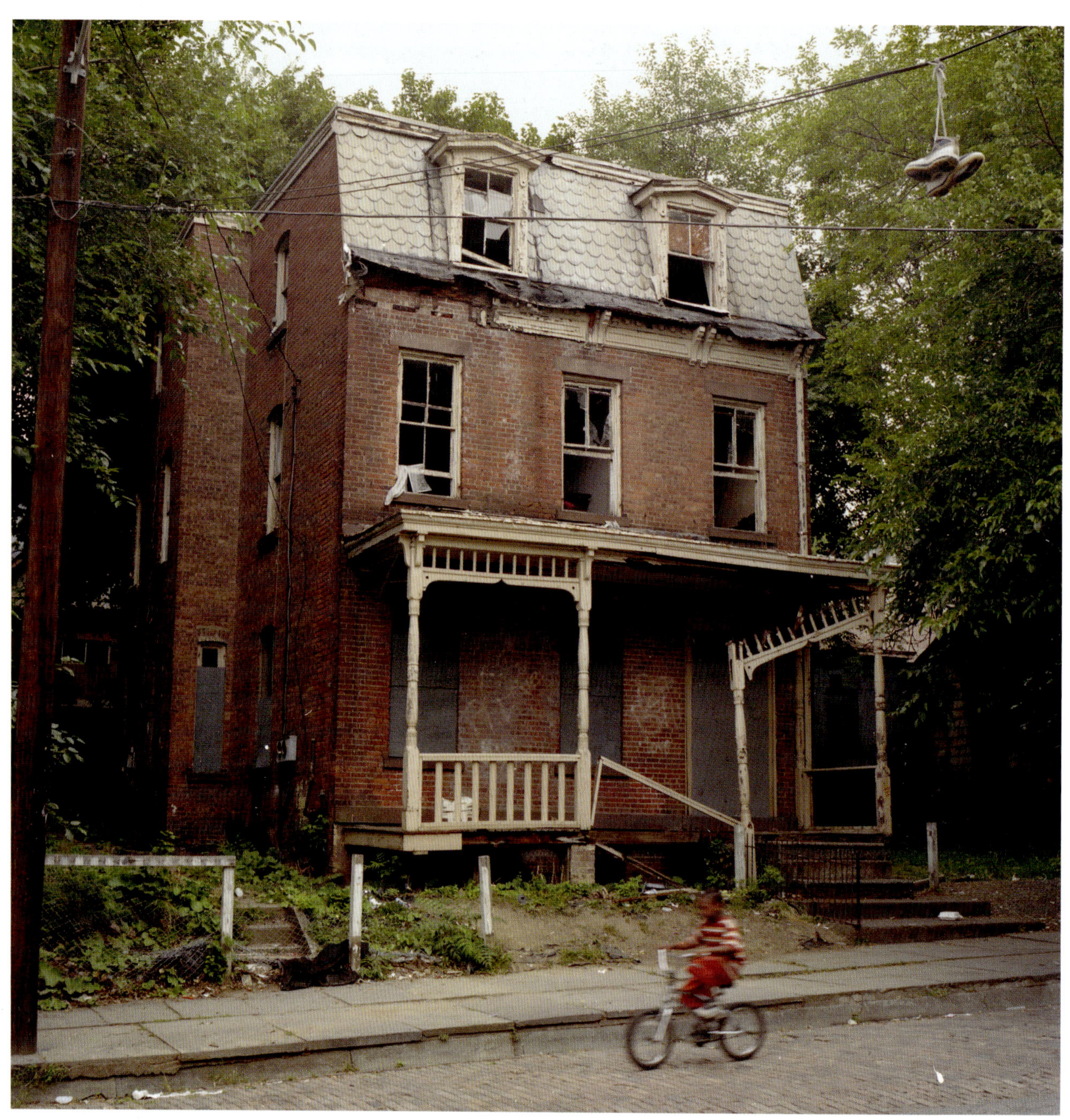

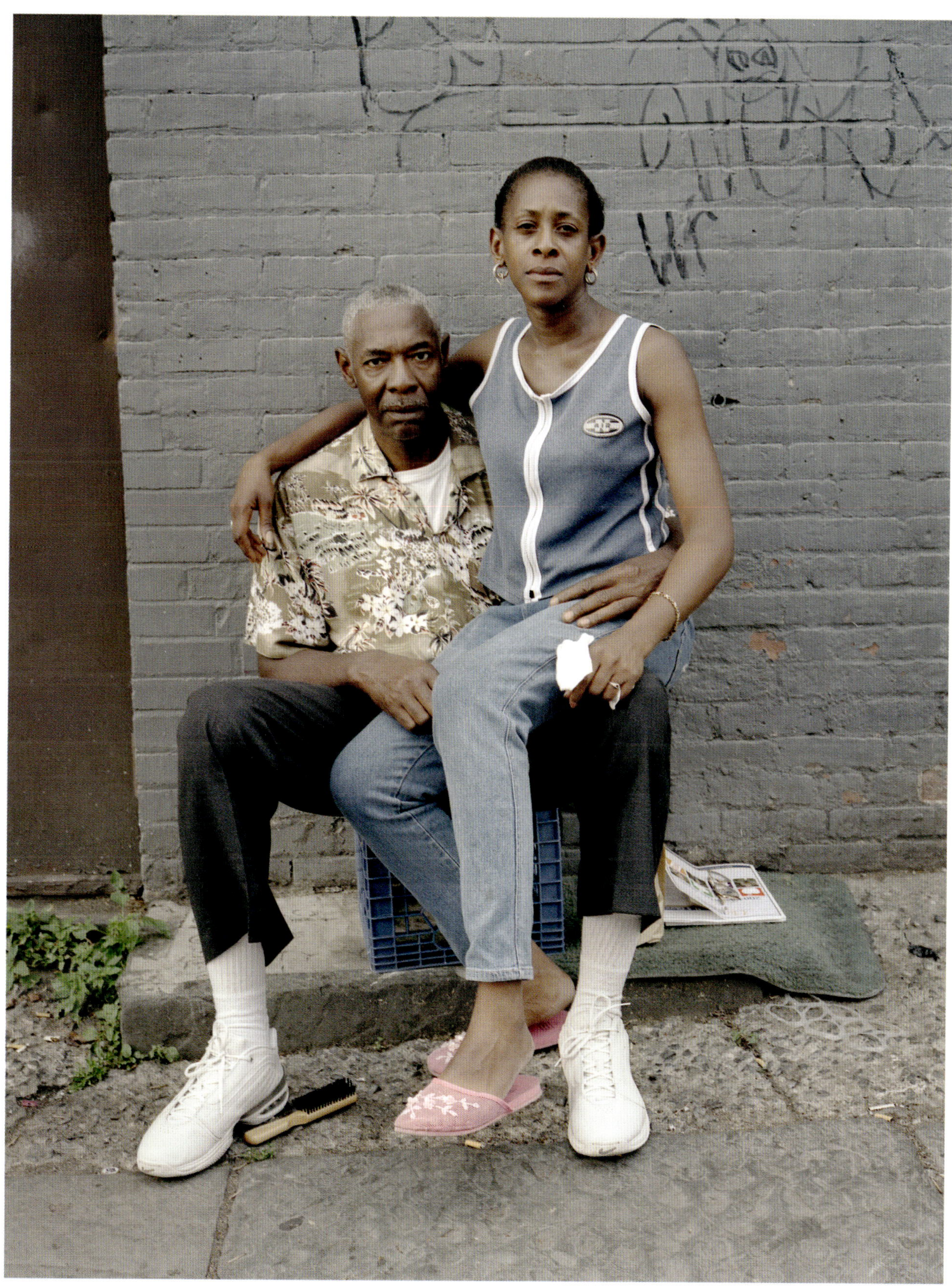

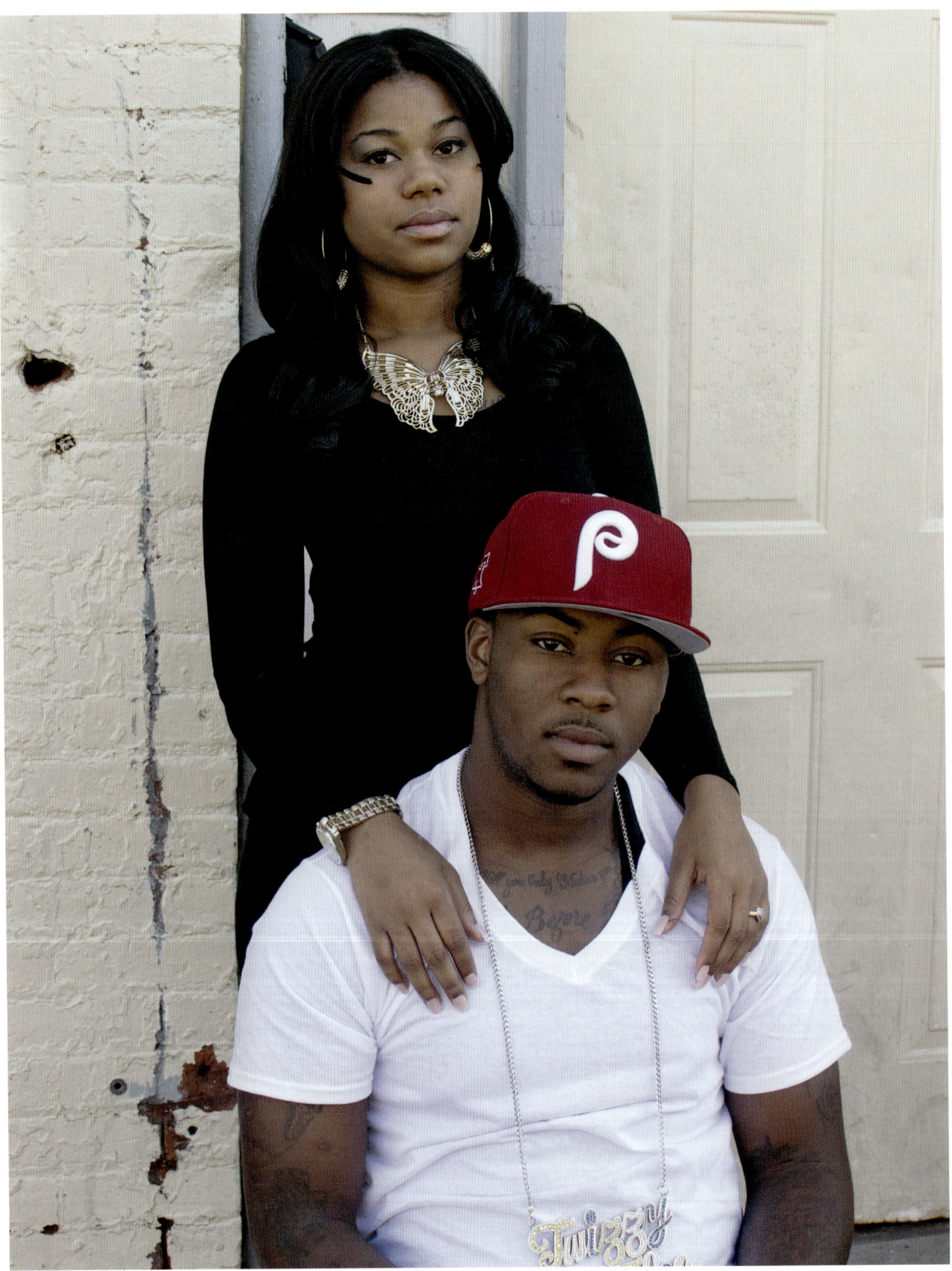
Twizzy

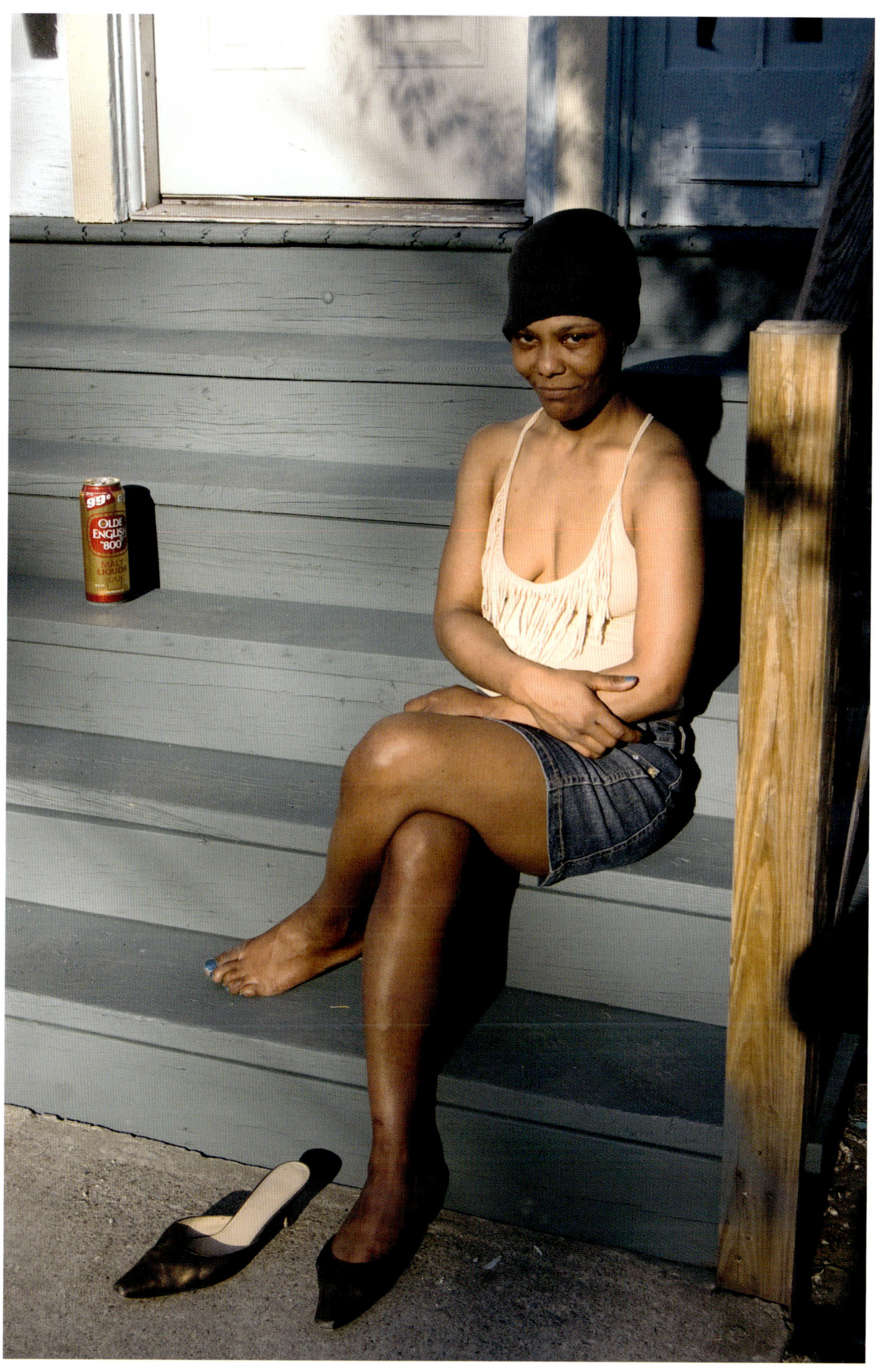
99¢
OLDE
"800"

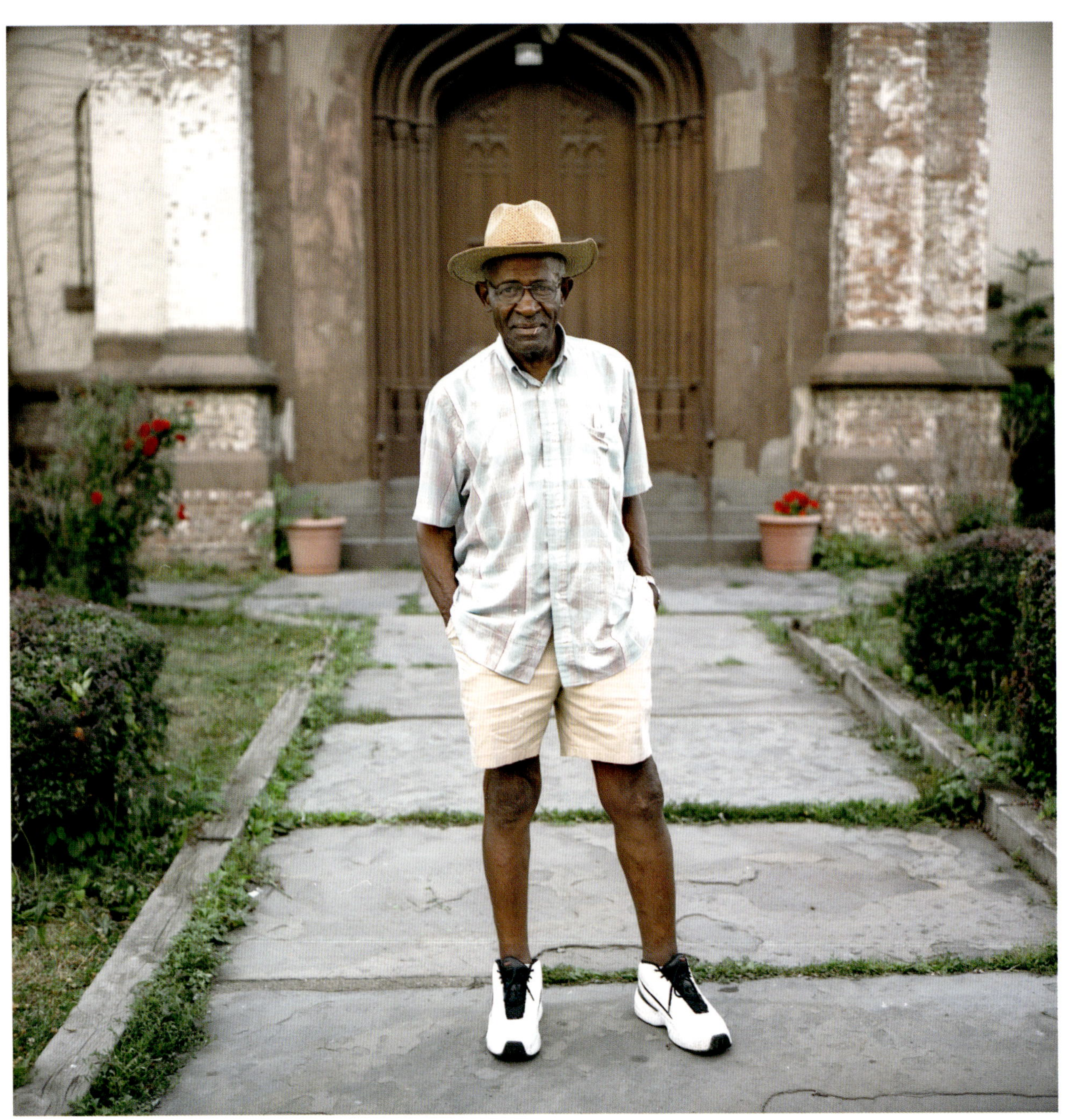

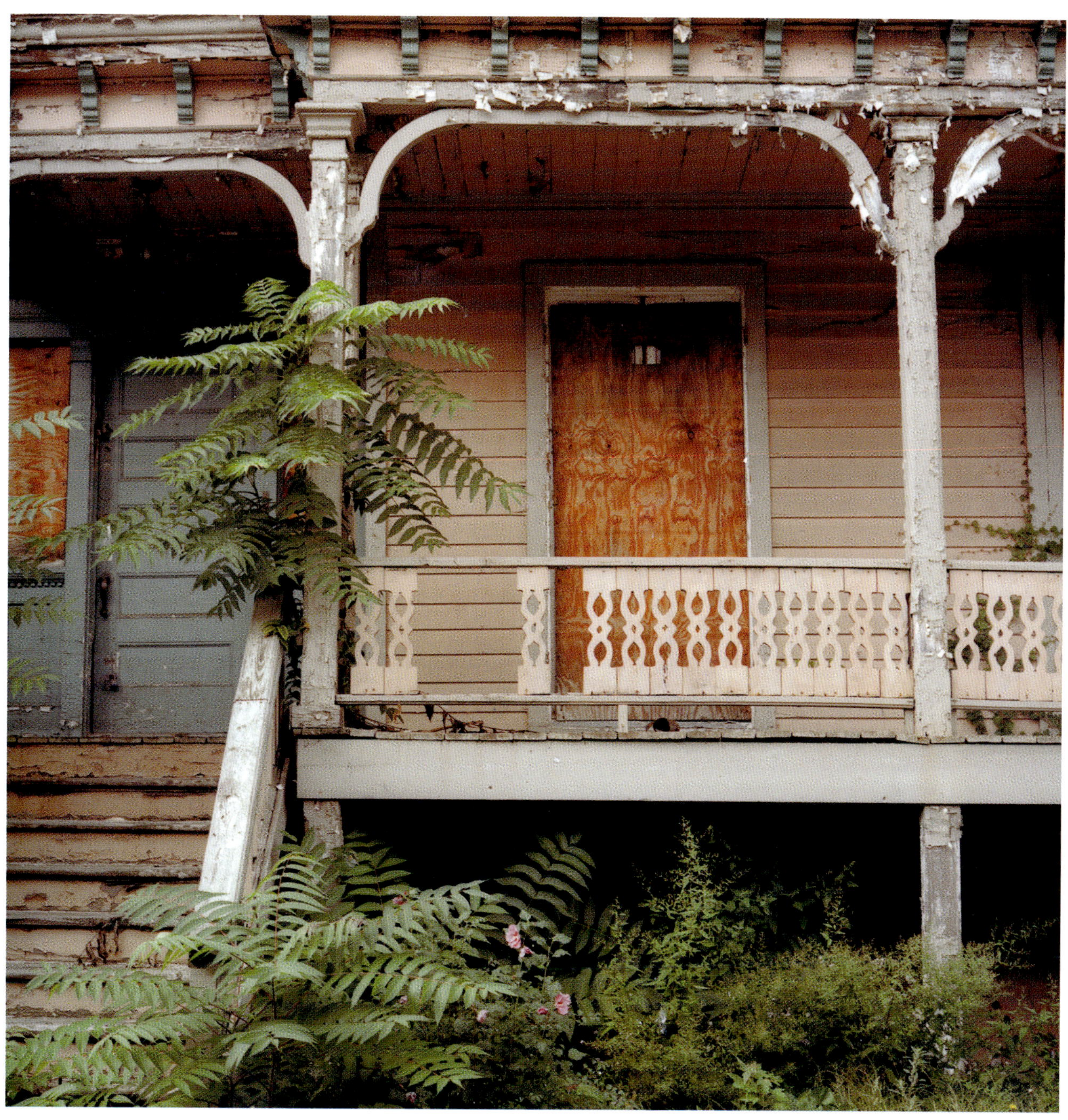

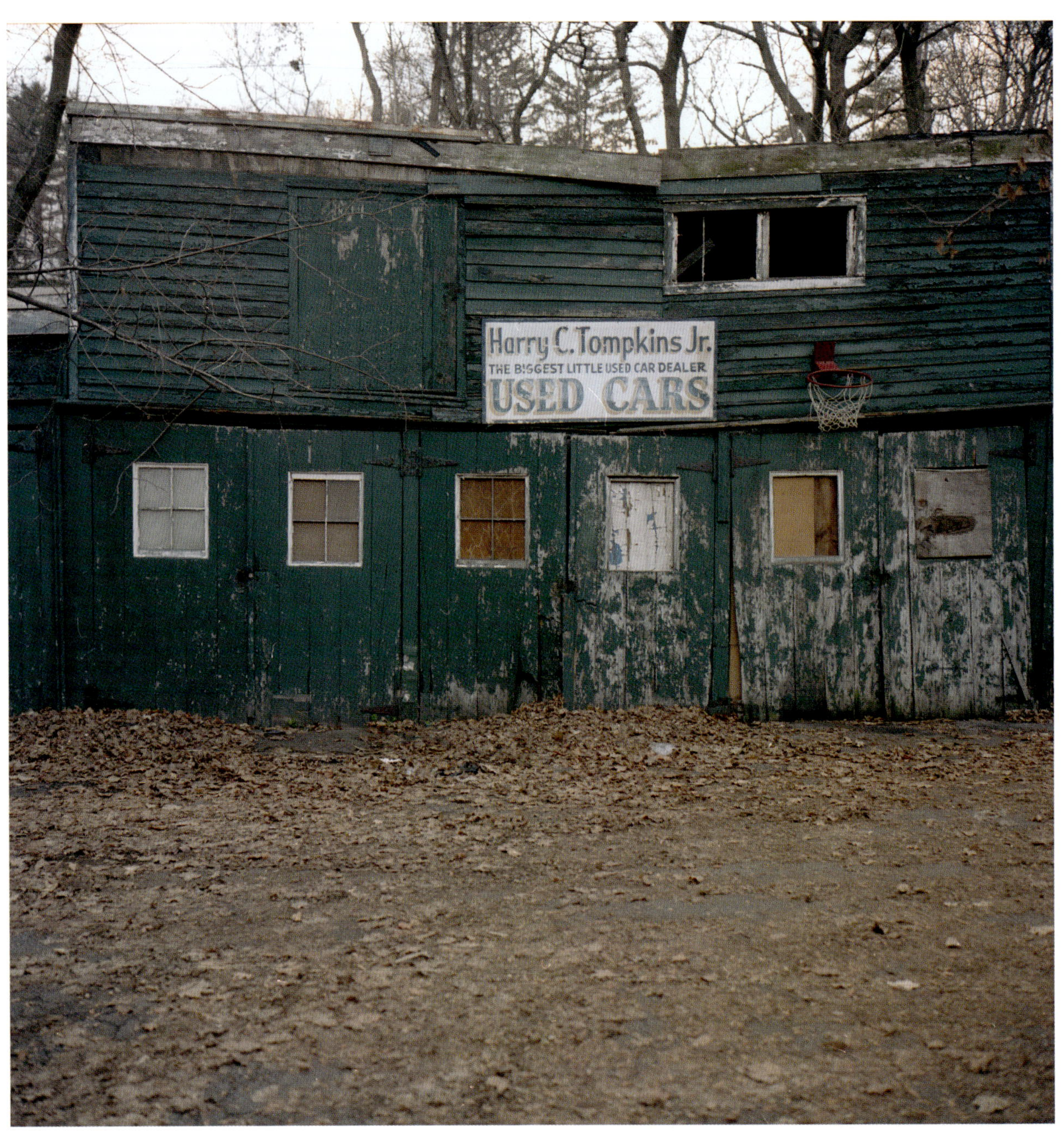
Harry C. Tompkins Jr.
THE BIGGEST LITTLE USED CAR DEALER
USED CARS

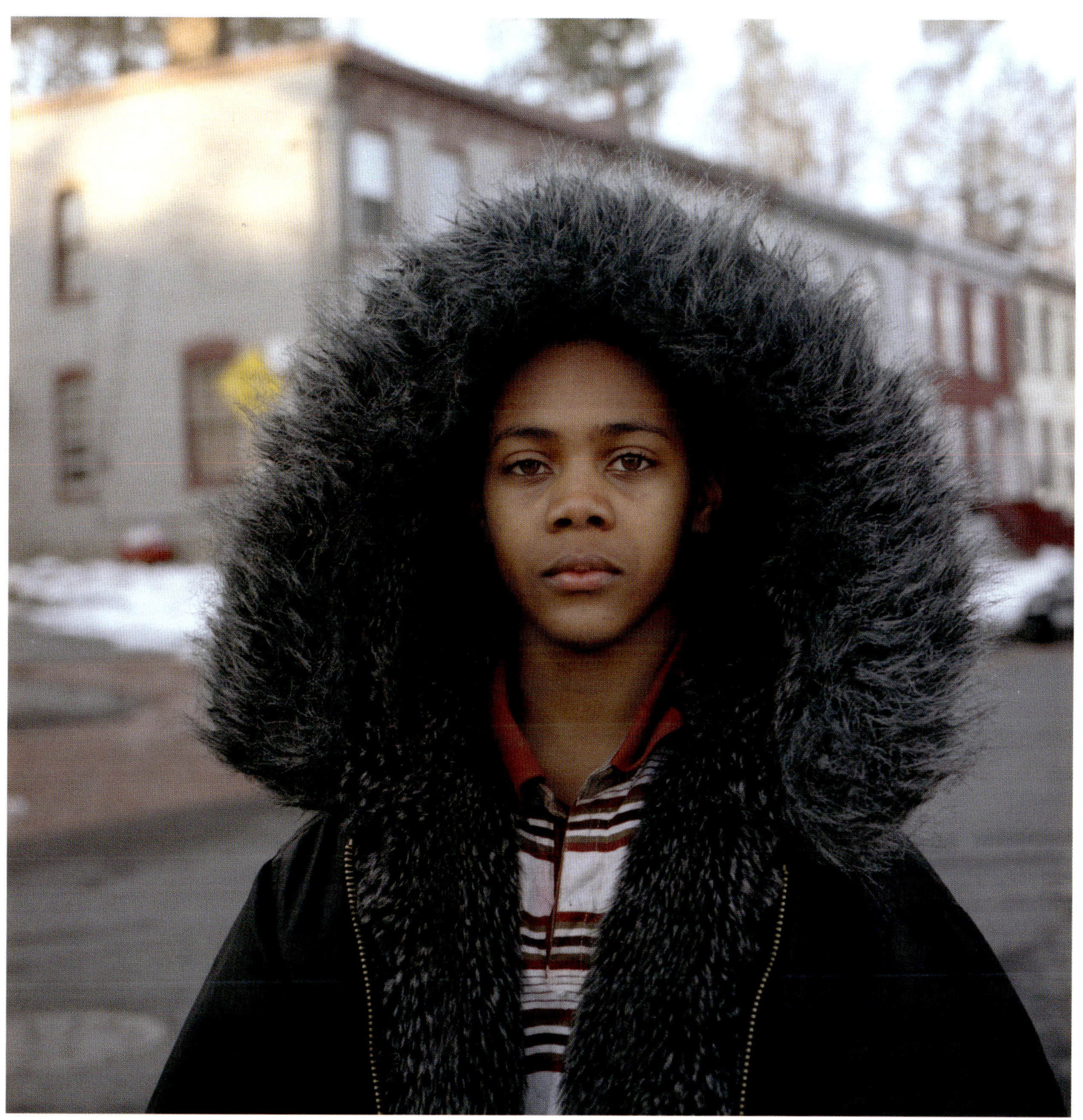

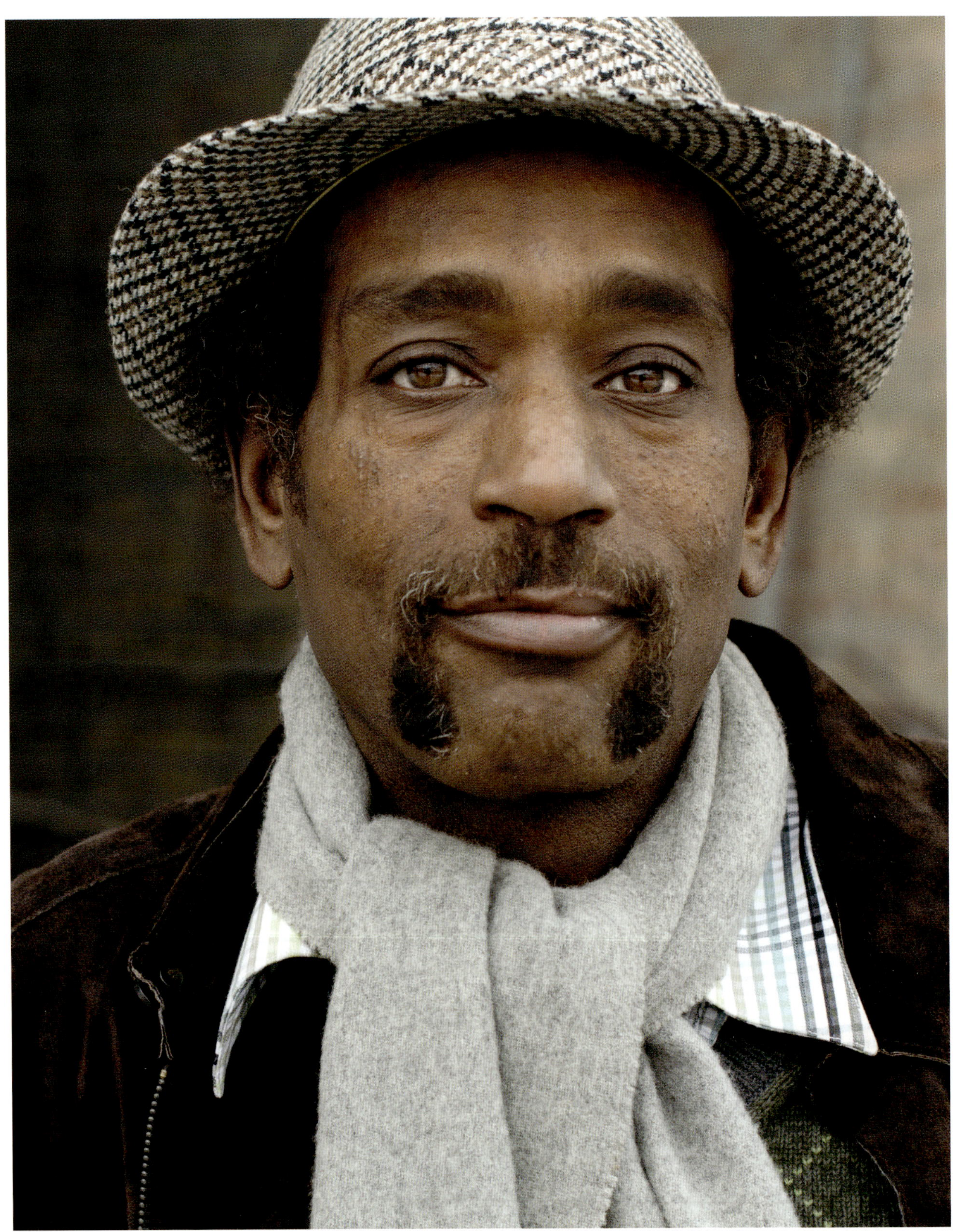

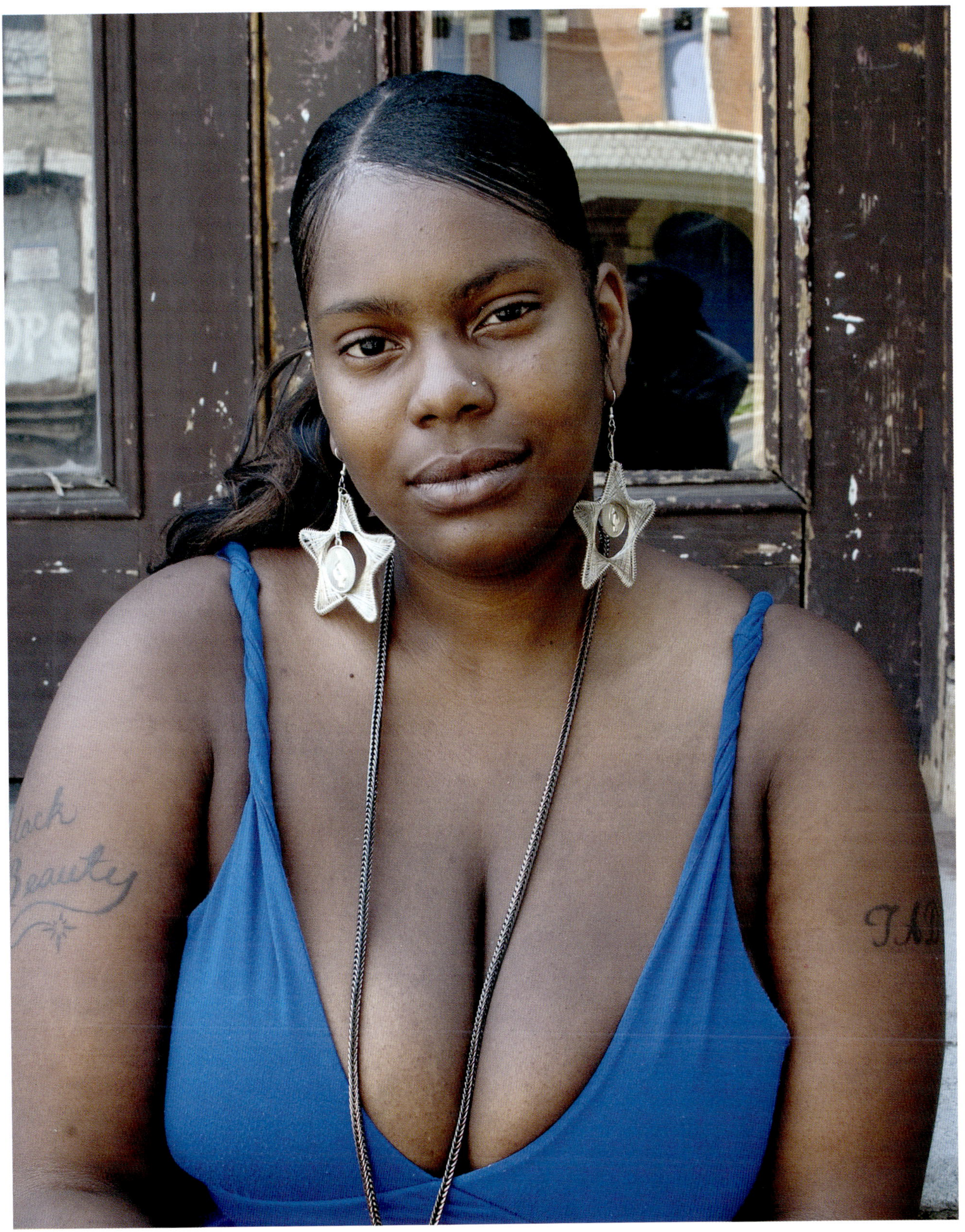

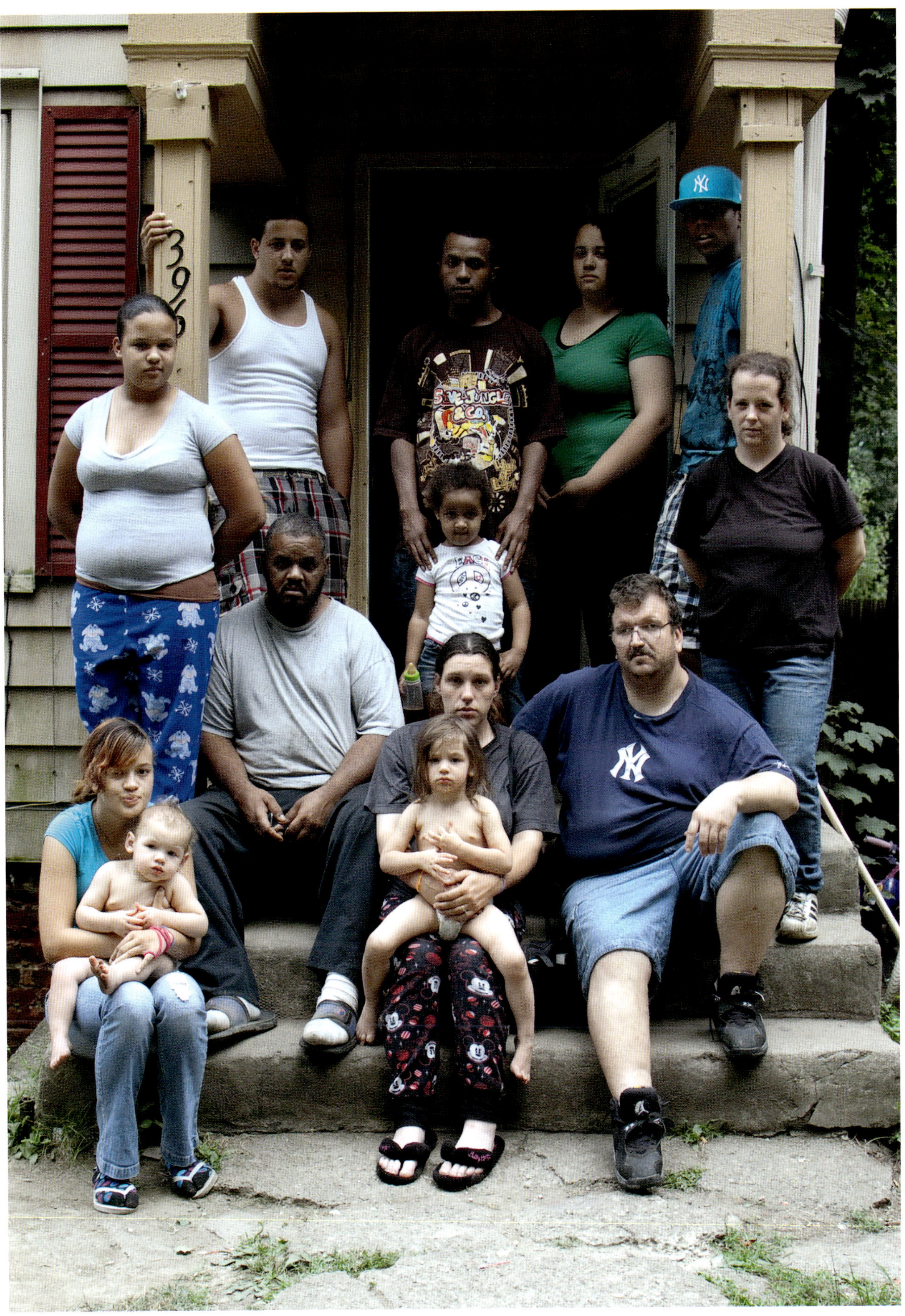

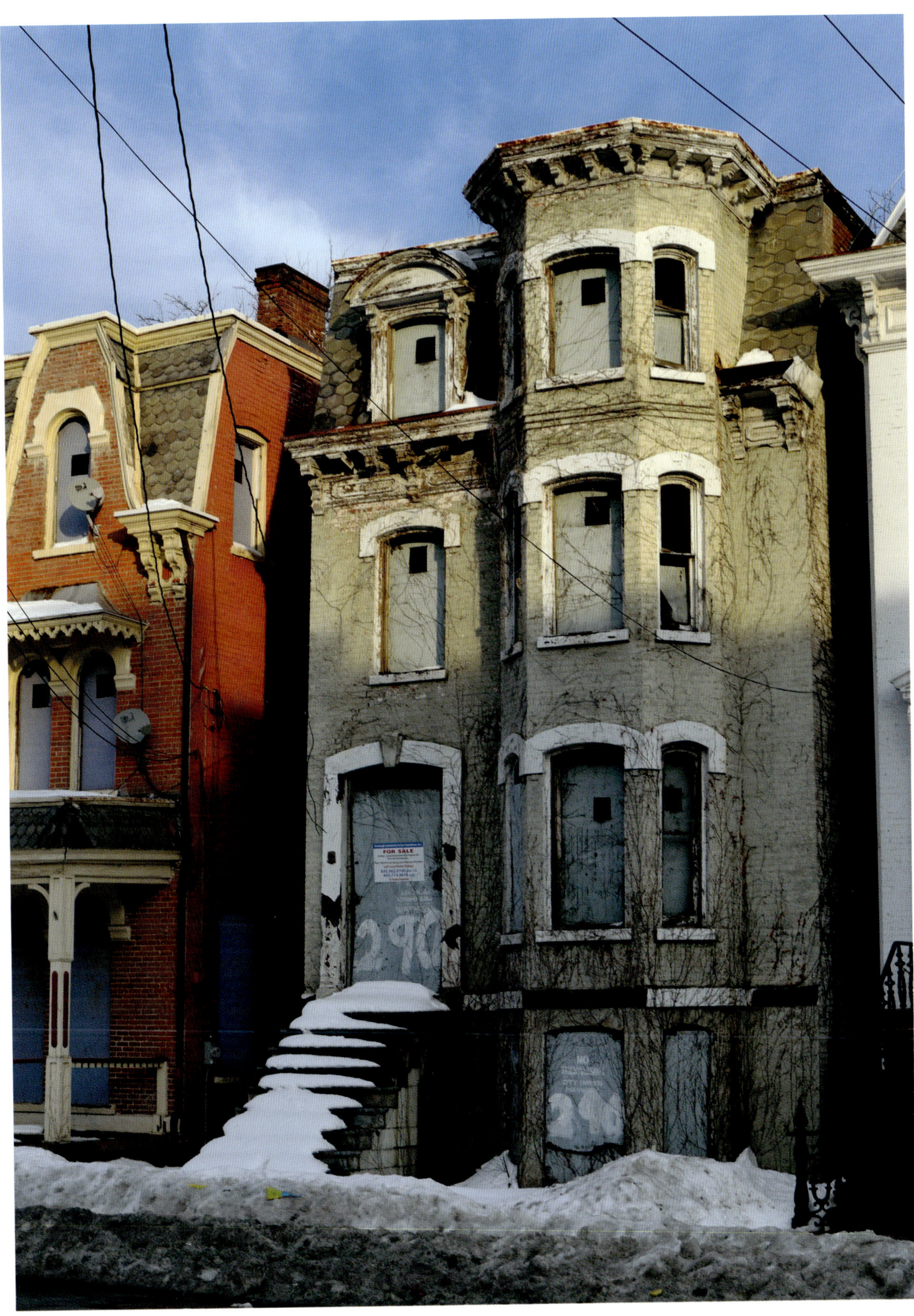
FOR SALE

PHOTOGRAPHER'S NOTES & ACKNOWLEDGMENTS

One raw February afternoon in 1996 I packed my camera bags and set out by car for Newburgh, a distance of approximately fifteen miles from my house in Garrison. It was one of many trips I made across the Hamilton Fish Bridge, which takes you from Beacon on the east bank of the Hudson River to Newburgh on the west. But it was my first trip with cameras and film and the intention to record the people and places of this crumbling and overlooked city. I was nervous; the start of a project is always uncertain. Would I see anything that I really wanted to photograph and would the people I wanted to photograph let me?

Before I finally decided to embark on this project, I made a number of trips to Newburgh and even one attempt at taking some photographs. My subject was not interested and told me to be on my way. But after each visit I always wanted to go back and look again. That February afternoon proved to be lucky—there were people I wanted to photograph and they agreed to be photographed. I came home with the picture of the girl in the silver quilted jacket (page 77). After such a promising start how could I not continue?

Standing on street corners with my favorite machine, a Rolleiflex 2.8E (circa 1955), attached to a Tiltall tripod, I stopped people and told them how wonderful they looked and asked if I could take their picture. Only a few said no; no money changed hands and a promise of a copy of the picture was made and kept wherever possible. I wandered the streets or looked in at the hotel, the barber's shop, or the corner store. For the close-up portraits I used my Hasselblad with a 150mm or 135mm lens.

I took the pictures almost always where I found my subjects, sometimes across the street to get out of the harsh sun or along here or over there to alter the background. Some people walked by muttering "no pictures" and sometimes they walked back and said, "Okay, then." I give the impression of being friendly and interested in my subjects, but while I am with my camera pointing it at them I see the person as a photograph, the finished print—that is what excites me. Some people want to talk a lot, which can interfere with getting the picture done, so I ask them to be quiet and talk to me later. I love the quiet people—I feel I can take my time—or the people who see at once what I am trying to do.

This is a record of uncelebrated and ignored people. The miserable start that most of the young in Newburgh have had, and the constant unemployment that their parents have endured since the 1950s, give many of the subjects an underlying sadness. But in the ruins of the buildings and in the faces of the people I see warmth and beauty, and in some of the faces a determination to change things.

I am grateful to John and Tamara Benjamin, Kim Connor, Emily Dupree, Alice Rose George, Nick Groombridge, Earle I. Mack, Teresa Quinn, and Carole Wolf, and to the Mill Street Loft in Poughkeepsie, New York.

Dmitri Kasterine